**Poverty, Politics and Race
(The View From Down Here)**

**Poverty, Politics and Race
(The View From Down Here)**

"Poverty, Politics, and Race"

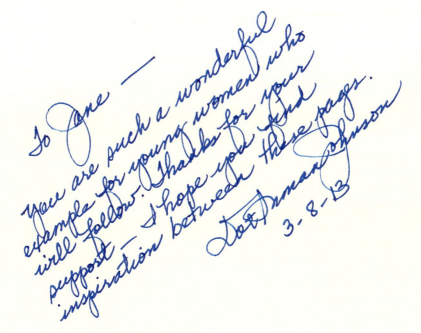

To Jane —
You are such a wonderful example for young women who will follow. Thanks for your support — I hope you find inspiration between these pages.
Hat Inman Johnson
3-8-13

Poverty, Politics and Race
(The View From Down Here)

**Poverty, Politics and Race
(The View From Down Here)**

Poverty, Politics, and Race

The View from Down Here

Dorothy Inman-Johnson

**Poverty, Politics and Race
(The View From Down Here)**

Poverty, Politics, and Race

Copyright © 2012 by Dorothy Inman-Johnson

All rights reserved. No part of this work may be reproduced or transmitted in any form or by any means. Electronic or mechanical, including photocopying and recording, or by any information storage or retrieval system, except as may be expressly permitted by the 1976 Copyright Act or in writing from the author. Request for permission should be addressed in writing via Amazon.com or to the address below.

> Dorothy Inman-Johnson
> P.O. Box 16607
> Tallahassee, Florida 32317

ISBN-13: 978-1481185660

Printed in the United States of America

Poverty, Politics and Race
(The View From Down Here)

**Poverty, Politics and Race
(The View From Down Here)**

**Poverty, Politics and Race
(The View From Down Here)**

Dedicated

To

Eugene and Helen Lee

Parents who sacrificed so much to create opportunities for me

And

Suzanne McDaniel

Who is like a mother to me

**Poverty, Politics and Race
(The View From Down Here)**

**Poverty, Politics and Race
(The View From Down Here)**

Table of Contents

Acknowledgments 1

Preface 4

Growing Up Poor 9

Chapter 2 21

Who Are The Poor? 21

Chapter 3 43

The Rules Are Different For Minorities and
the Poor 43

Chapter 4 53

The Role of Government 53

Chapter 5 75

Perspective from the Past 75

Chapter 6 85

**Poverty, Politics and Race
(The View From Down Here)**

Racial Hatred and the Church 85

Chapter 7 94

The Real Class Warfare 94

Chapter 8 104

Leveling the Credit Playing Field 104

Chapter 9 118

Environmental Justice 118

Chapter 10 130

The Survival of Public Education 130

Chapter 11 145

The Truth about Head Start 145

Chapter 12 157

Unions (Heroes of the Middle Class and Poor)
.... 157

Chapter 13 172

**Poverty, Politics and Race
(The View From Down Here)**

Romney Campaign: A Violation of Trust.....172

Chapter 14...186

President Obama – Breaking Down Barriers
....186

Chapter 15...201

Politicizing the U.S. Supreme Court................201

Chapter 16...209

Voter Suppression – An Assault on Democracy...209

Chapter 17...224

The Death of News 224

Final Thoughts..244

The 2012 Election..244

**Poverty, Politics and Race
(The View From Down Here)**

Acknowledgments

When in 2011, a year before my retirement, I started saying out loud instead of just thinking I would write the book that I had been carrying in my heart and mind, the people I love most never doubted I would do it. Reverend Lee Johnson, my wonderful husband, kept me inspired throughout the process, created a separate office space as a suitable environment for writing, and was my most reliable sounding board and constant support. W. Ann Lee, the youngest of my thirteen siblings and the one with whom I had shared most of the important events of my life, greeted my announcement with excitement and enthusiastic support. Since I am much more comfortable and more fluent writing in long hand instead of typing, Ann gladly took over transforming my handwritten pages to word documents, along with preliminary editing. All along the way, Lee and Ann pushed me to stay focused and kept me encouraged. It was Lee who refined the title. Without the extraordinary support of my husband and sister to stay focused, it would have been difficult to maintain the discipline required to complete **Poverty, Politics, and Race.**

Poverty, Politics and Race
(The View From Down Here)

My sons, Victor Inman and Sam Inman, greeted the news that I was writing a book with pride and approval. They willingly took over the typing responsibilities during a short period when their Aunt Ann's job requirements temporarily made her unavailable. I recognized my late father and mother, Eugene and Helen Lee, in the book's dedication, first, because I still love them so. Second, because it was their unselfish love, sacrifice, strength, and dedication to a better life for their children that made me the strong woman I became. Despite all the difficulties of their lives, most of the time they managed to make life so much fun, we could almost forget we were poor.

There was another dedication. It was to Suzanne McDaniel "who is like a mother to me". Actually, Mama Suzanne is my husband's aunt and the last surviving sibling of his mother who died in his youth. She has become more of a mother to him than an aunt; and since he first took me to meet her, I have felt that same special love. She's lovable, intellectually sharp, outrageously funny, and the most youthful eighty-six year old I have ever met. She makes you happy just being around her. I feel so blessed to have her in my life.

Other important people to thank are Judy Duchatkiewicz, affectionately known as Judy D mainly because we had trouble pronouncing her last name, for her invaluable contributions to the chapter on Head Start; Diane Haggerty and Michael Moody, who helped to compile pictures from old files; and Cynthia Valencic, an excellent fact checker on the Agency-run safety net programs. Very special thanks are extended to Crystal

**Poverty, Politics and Race
(The View From Down Here)**

Cleveland, an extraordinary young woman, for technical support in the submission of the work for publication. And, finally, for everyone who shared encouragement and believed that the book was possible, I sincerely thank each of you.

**Poverty, Politics and Race
(The View From Down Here)**

Preface

I was tired of listening to well meaning and sometimes not so well meaning and ill informed, TV talking heads on poverty and racism who have no firsthand experience or understanding of these issues. Having been born into poverty in Birmingham, a city that defined racism in the South, and having spent a big portion of my life overcoming those barriers and helping others do likewise, I decided it was important to add the perspective of those of us whose lives have been shaped by poverty, racism, and the political response to both.

Those most often given the public platform to speak on these issues have usually dealt with them from the perspective of a statistician or an observer who stands apart and reflects on what is seen and not felt. It is hard to know the damage to the psyche of a person or race of people who started their lives treated as second or third class citizens

Poverty, Politics and Race
(The View From Down Here)

and had this treatment passed down through generations, if you have not experienced it or spent a sizable amount of uninterrupted time with those who have.

I, therefore, have a great respect for Barbara Ehrenreich, author of <u>Nickel and Dimed</u>; because instead of making assumptions about life lived in poverty from a safe distance, she gave up her comfortable life and actually lived on sub-minimum or minimum wage jobs for months. She voluntarily placed herself in the same impoverished circumstances as the hotel and motel housekeeping staff and waitresses in the Conch Republic of Key West and those on minimum or sub minimum wage jobs in other parts of the country.

Her firsthand accounts of the desperation faced each day gave more legitimacy to her portrayal than any pollster's takeaway assumptions based on questions answered by a random samples of Americans giving their opinions on these important issues.

The results of polls are dependent on the questions asked, who is included in the sample of Americans being polled, the sample size, and what is happening during that moment in time. Polls are not about truth or justice, and have no ability to predict the impact of unusual circumstances on outcomes. Polls only provide a peek into opinions, biases, and perspectives of a specific group of people for that specific moment. Therefore, different polls

Poverty, Politics and Race
(The View From Down Here)

done on the same day by different pollsters on the same subject can render very different results.

Poverty and victimization by racism are not momentary conditions. Nor are their impacts easily cured or dismissed. Just imagine what the results of a poll would have been if we had been dependent on that poll to move forward on the Civil Rights or Voting Rights Act in the mid 1960s.

The outcome of such a poll would be questionable even today with the strong Tea Party influence on the Republican Party, which has led many of them to question the continuing need for both of those landmark laws in 2012. Studies over a much longer period of time, though limited by the control and research group, provide far more insight into cause and effect and establish real patterns of behavior. However, neither polling nor focus groups can compare in developing reliable data in these areas unless they include a fair sample of those most directly impacted over a lifetime.

Being frustrated with stereotypes regularly used to describe the poor, much more open displays of racism since the election of the first African-American President in 2008, and America's refusal to acknowledge this dynamic, I felt compelled to add my perspective to this ongoing dialogue. It allowed me to redirect my energy and frustration into writing **Poverty, Politics, and Race: The View From Down Here,** which was far preferable to finding relief by throwing objects or screaming at my TV. It has been a much more healthy response, as well.

Poverty, Politics and Race
(The View From Down Here)

Further, hate has become more openly expressed by certain segments of the population in this country, as demonstrated by the hateful disrespect toward President Obama and attempts to deny or roll back Constitutionally guaranteed rights to African-Americans, Hispanic Americans, women, gay Americans, as well as the poor since 2009. For those reasons, I felt a real urgency to give a voice to those usually not represented at the table when issues impacting their lives are discussed.

That voice is not one of a victim. Though the poor, women, minorities and LGBT Americans are often victimized by those in power, the battle is already lost when we start seeing ourselves as victims instead of as people with the power to determine our own destiny by joining forces and exercising the power found in numbers, when there is a common purpose.

Poverty, Politics, and Race _The View from Down Here is not the view of a pollster in which the result may change with each new poll based on the questions asked and the people polled. It is not the view of those who have had no first hand encounter with poverty, and racism. Nor is it the view of those who have never experienced the negative impacts of a political system controlled by the overwhelming influence of money, made even worse by the U.S. Supreme Court's Citizens United ruling.

It is clearly from the perspective of a big tent, inclusive, lifelong Democrat who happens to be a Black female as well. It is the direct opposite of the "survival of the fittest" philosophy in which

Poverty, Politics and Race
(The View From Down Here)

those with the power and money take home the spoils and the rest of America is left on a starvation diet. The wide gap in income between the wealthiest in this country and middle to low-income residents is evidence that the Right's interpretation of the vision and promise of America runs counter to the intent of the Preamble of the Constitution "to promote the general welfare".

And, finally, this book is from the perspective of a proud American who has not forgotten from whence she came, and will not stand quietly by as the ugliness of America's past threatens to choke the life out of America's promise for all except the most wealthy and powerful among us.

**Poverty, Politics and Race
(The View From Down Here)**

Chapter 1

Growing Up Poor

Poverty, Politics and Race
(The View From Down Here)

I was the fifth child of 14 children of Eugene and Helen Lee who were among the "working poor". My early life was colored not just by our financial circumstances, but by the places where I grew up in Birmingham. First was Yellow Quarters – rows of shotgun houses dissected by dirt alleyways instead of paved streets. Yellow Quarters was near Tuxedo Junction in Ensley, on Birmingham's Westside.

I remember my parents' whispers about the Saturday night drunken brawls and a neighbor's stabbing death. This implies a danger from which my parents did their best to shield my siblings and me. Instead, my memories and family photo album have images of toddlers and pre-schoolers_ my brothers in tiny suits and the girls in starched, ruffled dresses and ribbons, holding Easter baskets before leaving for Easter Sunday Service at Abyssinia Missionary Baptist Church. It was the church where we were all baptized and my Dad was a deacon.

Yellow Quarters, and its rows of old, wooden, shotgun houses, was eventually replaced by the Tuxedo Housing Project, with its sparkling new 2, 3, 4, and 5 bedroom apartments. There was no stigma attached to living in subsidized housing then. The new Tuxedo Subsidized Housing Project was considered the answer to a prayer for many large families like ours crammed into a small 3 room house where all three rooms, including the front room and kitchen doubled as bedrooms.

Families lined up to apply to be among the first selected for a home large enough for their

Poverty, Politics and Race
(The View From Down Here)

family at a rent that they could afford. It was many years later, after I had moved to Atlanta for college, that my mother moved to the projects with my younger siblings. Instead, for me after Yellow Quarters, our next move was to Sandy Bottom during my early years in elementary school.

Sandy Bottom was a stone's throw from the Steel Mill that employed many of the residents and cast a large shadow over the 3-room houses on the street where we lived. Our front and backyards were never covered with the lush, green grass lawns we saw in the "Dick and Jane" books we read in our early school years. Our yard was grayish brown or black dirt; or thick, dark mud when it rained.

My strongest memory of the Sandy Bottom house was the day I came home from school to an empty house and found my Dad's bloody work clothes piled on the kitchen floor. Immediately the next door neighbor was there to hug me, carry me off to her house to join my siblings, and explain that our mother was at the hospital with my Dad. He had been injured on the job. That was my most vivid memory – the day I learned my Dad's hands had been crushed beneath a coal car as he worked on the rails in the Docena Coal Mine.

Though my Dad was a coal miner, his joy was the beautiful works of art he created with his hands. He could take a piece of wood and a pocket knife and after a few strategic cuts, an old man, an animal, or a magic box from which a beautifully colored snake curled forward when the lid was

Poverty, Politics and Race
(The View From Down Here)

pulled back. The things he could create with his hands seem magic.

He could repair or build almost anything. Those hands built the kind of playhouse for his little girls that wealthier families pay a fortune for today. He built unique furniture pieces for our home and caned chairs or recovered furniture for us and for neighbors for extra money to support his large family. The same hands made him the neighborhood barber and our back porch the neighborhood barbershop most Saturdays.

As children we marveled at his beautiful pencil and charcoal drawings. And, as Daddy's big girl, I was rewarded with a little drawing table and chair that allowed me to sit, watch, and draw beside him. At the time, we did not understand what a special and talented man he was. He was just our Daddy.

The mine accident robbed him of the use of both hands and his joy for life. He lost his three middle fingers and half the little finger on his right hand. He was right-handed. His left hand was crushed leaving the fingers on that hand permanently bent.

The Docena mine paid his hospital bill and laid him off with no benefits to cover his work related disability or income for his family. He was never the same after Sandy Bottom.

By the time we moved to Avenue S in Ensley, across from the Holy Family Hospital, my

Poverty, Politics and Race
(The View From Down Here)

parents were legally separated, but never divorced. We had moved up a slot to a 4 room double tenant rental, much like a duplex. Mom slept in the front room which doubled as our living room. The girls piled into a large bed in the next room, and all of the boys, 5 still at home at the time, all crowded into beds in the third room, leaving the small kitchen which was too small to fit even a rollaway bed.

There was no privacy or quiet place to read, do homework or just to be alone with your thoughts. I developed a habit of stealing away to the kitchen late at night when everyone else was asleep to draw, write, read or do homework. The habit stayed with me throughout life. My most productive time for concentrated projects in college and in my career has always been late at night when everyone else is tucked away in bed.

My mother, the primary bread winner by then, was up at 4:30 a.m. and had cleaned, washed a load of clothes, and had a hot breakfast on the table before she woke us to eat, clean our room and hang out the clothes on the line.

As soon as we were off to school, she walked the 3 to 4 miles to the home of the white family where she worked most of the rest of our childhood. She cleaned their house, washed and ironed their clothes, cooked their meals, and cared for their son and twin daughters – much like the maids portrayed in the 2011 movie "The Help". Unlike some of the relationships in the movie, however, it

Poverty, Politics and Race
(The View From Down Here)

was clear there was mutual caring and respect between my mother and her employers.

Their family's spring and fall cleaning was a bonanza for us. Reorganizing the children's closets meant Mom would be bringing home boxes of nice clothes in our size, since the twins were close in age and size to me and my two younger sisters. There were always two outfits exactly alike. Sometimes my sister Joyce and I dressed in twin outfits, and other times my two sisters were the twins. The family also often brought boxes of food and toys at Christmas time.

We attended segregated Council Elementary School, grades 1-8, and Western Olin High, grades 9-12. Though we had dedicated teachers, many who lived in the same community as their students, these schools hardly ever received adequate materials and never received the newly adopted textbooks, fresh off of the store or school warehouse book shelves. Our books came with the markings of previous owners and, often, with missing pages. The newly adopted or updated textbooks went to the all White Schools. The Black Schools received the hand-me-down, out-of-adoption books discarded by the White Schools. And despite the barriers, our parents insisted that we do our best in school because they saw a good education as a gateway to a better life for their children than the one they had.

My Dad only had a third grade education. He grew up on a farm in Union Springs, Alabama. When he completed third grade and was thought to

Poverty, Politics and Race
(The View From Down Here)

be big enough to help on the farm, his Dad pulled him out of school to help in the fields. He worked hard for most of the rest of his life at any honest job that allowed him to take care of his family.

My Mom's education ended at eighth grade. She also was no stranger to hard work. When she sent us off to school, she meant it when she said, "Mind your teachers and do your work". If one of the teachers had to call home because of misbehavior by one us, the switch she pulled from the willow tree in the yard was a painful reminder not to make that mistake again. She was always the disciplinarian in the household.

By now it's clear, my Mom was no shrinking violet – strong, hard working, smart, and full of fun, but with high expectations for her children. It was a regular summer activity to have neighborhood kids gathering for a stick ball game on the street in front of the houses lining our street. When we were very young, both my Mom and Dad played with a local baseball league, and sometimes the parents joined in with their children for a neighborhood stick ball game. I can remember sitting on the grass at the ball field cheering my Mom as she played with her women's league, and cheering my Dad's game afterward. It was these local league games, played for fun, which created some of the top Negro League players like my cousin, Willie James Lee, who played with the Kansas City Monarchs. The story of these early sports heroes is chronicled in the book titled, **Only The Ball Was White** by Robert Peterson.

Poverty, Politics and Race
(The View From Down Here)

Negro League Player Willie James Lee with the Kansas City Monarchs

Poverty, Politics and Race
(The View From Down Here)

Despite my mother's long work day, I cannot remember a day that we returned from school when a hot supper was not waiting for us. The meal may have been only a big pot of pinto beans with neck bones or salt pork, and corn bread hot from the oven, but it tasted good and we were never hungry.

My family's household size and income qualified us to receive USDA commodities, the federal emergency food distribution program for poor, elderly, and disabled households. The monthly food box usually included a huge block of cheese, large can of syrup, canned chipped beef, large bag of rice, flour, meal, sugar, dried beans, powdered milk and eggs, canned spam and peanut butter. The powdered milk and eggs tasted terrible, but Mom could do miracles in the kitchen by turning these commodities into delicious meals.

My mom, along with all Black-Americans, was prohibited from voting until the Voting Rights Act of 1965 went into effect. She, however, was not timid about her civil rights activism. After long days at work and caring for us, she somehow found the time to recruit neighbors with cars to join car pools transporting marchers and demonstrators to downtown Birmingham to volunteer for the peaceful demonstrations.

She also began taking us with her on Thursday nights to the rousing mass meetings at Birmingham's Sixteenth Street Baptist Church. Once there, we were energized and inspired by the excitement of the sermons and rallying speeches from that pulpit by Rev. Martin Luther King Jr.,

Poverty, Politics and Race
(The View From Down Here)

Rev. Ralph Abernathy, and Birmingham's own Rev. Fred Shuttlesworth. And, with my Mom's approval, we were among the youth to join the peaceful demonstrations and pickets in downtown Birmingham.

My mother, who did not learn to drive until she was in her late fifties, made it her commitment to recruit neighbors with cars for the car pools to ensure a regular flow of volunteers were being transported from Ensley to downtown Birmingham as fresh recruits. She also helped with preparation of meal breaks at the church for demonstrators.

Though there were threats to bomb the church, Thursday nights drew over-flow crowds to the mass meetings that regularly closed with joined hands and voices lifted in singing "We Shall Overcome". Soon I would leave home for college in Atlanta on a four year scholarship; but returned home my first summer to join other youth as volunteers in voter registration canvassing throughout Jefferson County. After the first summer, jobs to assist with my college expenses prevented my return to Birmingham to volunteer.

As soon as my Mom was allowed to register to vote, she did. It gave her such a sense of pride that for all of her life, even when old and with limited mobility, she insisted on walking into the polling place and casting her vote in person, rather than by absentee ballot.

My mother, like many of the parents in my childhood, came of age without any of the

Poverty, Politics and Race
(The View From Down Here)

opportunities youth today take for granted; but they wanted much more for their children. Though she only had an 8th grade education, she constantly preached education as the path to good job opportunities, and living life on our own terms. My mother was the perfect example of a strong, intelligent, and independent woman.

The woman I am today is a combination of the wonderful things learned from both parents but in greater part from my mother.

And my life in Birmingham, as a child, speaks to many of the problems we have today between the "haves" and "have nots"; and between those with power and the disenfranchised. The example of my family speaks to hard working parents struggling to care for, protect, and provide opportunities for a better life for their children. It hints at many of the generational barriers and some of the injustices covered in this book that face minorities and the poor even today. They include poor access to affordable, quality housing, fair and livable wages and benefits, opportunities for a quality education regardless of income status, and protection of hard won rights under the Constitution.

As my family's story shows, low-income families are no different than other families, except in the resources available to them and the barriers operating against them. Most struggle everyday to provide the basic needs for their families in caring homes, under very difficult circumstances, sometimes in more dangerous neighborhoods. The

Poverty, Politics and Race
(The View From Down Here)

biggest take away from my story, though, should be the normal routine of our family's life in spite of the adversities, instead of the stereotypes that so easily roll off the tongues of politicians like Newt Gingrich, Rick Santorum, and Florida Governor Rick Scott who required all applicants for Food Stamps or public assistance to be drug tested. Obviously, the Governor and the Florida Republican-controlled Legislature believed there was a direct correlation between poverty and drug addiction.

Stories of real low-income families tear down these stereotypes that the right wing political machine often uses to marginalize the poor. Instead, such stories reveal the complex layers of poor families' lives that match the complexities of the lives of all Americans. Hopefully, understanding that will make it harder in the future to divide people of different ethnicities, cultures, lifestyles, and incomes into "them" and "us".

**Poverty, Politics and Race
(The View From Down Here)**

Chapter 2

Who Are The Poor?

Poverty, Politics and Race
(The View From Down Here)

References are regularly made to poor Americans as though they are a monolith of lazy, irresponsible slugs who expect others to take care of them. GOP Presidential candidate Mitt Romney famously made the following statement to a group of wealthy campaign donors, at a supposed very private $50,000 a plate fundraising event.

"There are 47% of the people who will vote for the President no matter what. All right, there are 47% who are with him, who are dependent upon government, who believe they are victims, who believe the government has a responsibility to care for them, who believe that they are entitled to healthcare, to food, to housing, to you name it. That that's an entitlement. And the government should give it to them. And they will vote for this president no matter what. These are people who pay no income tax.... My job is not to worry about these people. I'll never convince them they should take personal responsibility and care for their own lives"

On the **Up w/ Chris Hayes** MSNBC show, September 23, 2012, a Romney Economic Advisor Emil Henry tripled down on Romney's statement and added "President Obama presides over 46 million Americans on food stamps as opposed to 10 million over a decade ago." I would venture a guess that Henry was likely one of the advisors who prepared that ill-advised statement for Romney. He went on to state, "Of course, he's (Romney) a good people person", when questioned about Romney's

Poverty, Politics and Race
(The View From Down Here)

inability to connect with the plight of regular Americans.

I say, of course, he's a good people person with rich people like him; those able to pay $50,000 a plate to hear him cater to their basest instincts by unfairly demeaning almost half of the American people.

Chris, correctly, fact checked Henry by pointing out that of the 47% Romney calls moochers off of the system_ 60% pay as much as 16% of their earnings in payroll taxes (Medicare and social security). Or they are people who are just so poor _ earning minimum wage on part-time or temporary jobs _ that the income tax does not apply. Further, the Earned Income Tax Credit (EITC), passed under President Bush and the Child Tax Credit are the reasons many of the poor in the 47% do not pay income taxes.

However undeterred by facts, Henry's statement that Americans on food stamps increased from 10% under Republicans to 46% under President Obama_ to feed the GOP myth that Obama is the "Food Stamp President"_ deserved a quick correction. And Chris did just that by reporting the number of Americans on Food Stamps (SNAP) rose to 32% under Bush. Henry very conveniently neglected to acknowledge that it was Bush economic policies that caused America to be bleeding almost 800,000 jobs a month on the day Barack Obama was sworn in as President. Those policies were also the major cause of the increase in

Poverty, Politics and Race
(The View From Down Here)

the percent of Americans receiving Food Stamps and living in desperate poverty.

During the Bush administration, the income gap between the rich and poor rose to record levels, with little notice until recently. It is commendable that America continues its role as an international leader in improving the lives of the poor in third world nations. It is as important, however, that at least as much attention and resources are dedicated to the poor in this country.

Though most pundits took issue with just the arrogance of Romney, a presidential candidate, openly proclaiming it would not be his job _ if elected _ to worry about 47% of Americans who did

Poverty, Politics and Race
(The View From Down Here)

not support him, it was another part of his statement that caught my attention. That statement was, "they believe that they are entitled to healthcare, to food, to housing, you- name- it...." It demonstrated an incredible lack of sensitivity and total disdain for those less fortunate.

I have worked at part time jobs since I was a teenager, and worked in my profession as an educator, non-profit administrator, and advocate for better opportunities for the poor for 43 years, until my retirement in May 2012. Over that period, as an average middle income earner, I certainly paid my fair share of federal income taxes, Medicare, and social security taxes _ while raising my family and having as much concern as anyone about the future of my precious grandchildren. There are fourteen of them who range in age from two 21 year old college students on Pell Grants and student loans to two infant granddaughters. Like most Americans, we want to build an America full of promise and even more opportunities than we had. But we do not feel those opportunities are only possible by denying the poorest among us resources for their basic needs.

Unlike Mitt Romney and his wealthy buddies, I certainly feel that America's poor should be able to expect help from taxes paid to the federal government by me and other Americans for access to healthcare, food, and a roof over their head, in times of need. That's the least a nation as wealthy as ours can do for its most vulnerable. Romney, Henry, and the ultra-right wing of the GOP seem to have an attitude about the poor that is personified by the statement attributed to Marie Antoinette,

Poverty, Politics and Race
(The View From Down Here)

"Let them eat cake" when told there was no bread for the hungry.

Everyone has heard the stereotypes about the poor _ "welfare queens", "food stamp frauds", "lazy moochers_ instead of the truth that most are hard working Americans, too old and sick to work any longer, disabled, or children.

The poor are referred to as the "working poor" for a good reason. Despite their efforts to take care of their households on minimum wage, and sometimes sub-minimum wage jobs, they still fall below the federal poverty guideline for their household size. They make up 60% of the 47% of Americans for whom Romney would have felt no obligation to worry about as President. Thirty percent (30%) are the elderly who worked hard until their later years and paid federal taxes, social security, and Medicare taxes for the services low-income seniors depend upon now that they are no longer able to work. The remaining ten percent (10%) are either active military for whom federal income taxes are waived, or Americans who are so poor and low on the income scale that they do not qualify to pay income tax.

How much of a Scrooge do the rich have to be to expect an impoverished family living in a dilapidated, single-wide mobile home with rotted floors, to pay more taxes so the rich will not be required to pay a penny more? Or even worse, they wanted a 10% lower tax rate for the rich to be paid for by heaping added financial burdens on the backs

Poverty, Politics and Race
(The View From Down Here)

of poor children and elderly Americans. Have they no shame?!

Maybe they envy the disabled, over 60 year old elderly woman who came to a social service organization in tears, feeling hopeless that despite her many years of work, she found herself on social security disability with a monthly income of $700, and her rent alone at $600 monthly. She was left with $100 to cover all her other basic needs for food, medicine, and utilities an absolutely impossible expectation. Her utilities had been off for a week before being referred to the Agency by the utility company. The agency was a recipient of the federal Low-Income Home Energy Assistance Program (LIHEAP) to assist low-income Americans pay their utility and fuel oil costs.

Thanks to the LIHEAP safety net program, this financially overwhelmed, disabled American not only received help getting her utility bill paid, but was referred to a case worker for the Agency's Family Self Sufficiency Program _ funded by another federal safety net program, Community Services Block Grant _ that assisted her to find and relocate to more affordable housing, apply for food stamps, and certify to receive monthly commodities. This low-income American clearly was not a welfare queen, nor was she engaged in food stamp fraud. She was not lazy and happy to live off of the rest of us. She was experiencing financial and health problems beyond her control and had the right to expect that an America that is among the first countries to help other poor nations would not turn its back on the poor in our own country.

Poverty, Politics and Race
(The View From Down Here)

And neither was the elderly veteran a moocher, who had lived for decades in the same small house that had been home to his family long before a city grew up around him. His house was built at a time when building and health codes did not require indoor plumbing. And no one would have known in 2000 he still did not have it if he had not applied to the local Urban League for emergency home repair. His circumstance, revealed during a poverty tour, became the subject of a newspaper article and brought attention to the plight of many poor residents living in similar conditions.

No one even imagined that this veteran who had given so much to his country was living in a home in the middle of an urban neighborhood with no indoor plumbing. The City had grown up over the many decades since his house was built, and left him behind. The tour revealed deep pockets of poverty in the community that resulted in the mobilization of governmental and community resources to totally remodel his home and improve conditions for many more poor residents.

**Poverty, Politics and Race
(The View From Down Here)**

Inman-Johnson (June 4, 2000) Poverty's hidden until we look Tallahassee Democrat p3E

Yet the wealthy corporate leaders, enjoying their $50,000 meal at the Romney event where the poor were being disparaged, felt it was a drain on their bank accounts and investments to pay a little more in taxes to provide free or reduced priced breakfast and lunches for the many poor children who arrive at schools all over America each morning hungry. The federally funded School breakfast and lunch program often provides the most reliable and nutritious meals very poor children receive. Without this program, many children would be unable to concentrate in school because of the noise and hunger pains from their empty stomachs.

The wealthy Wall Street types though comfortable with the subprime mortgage industry that caused so many mortgage foreclosures_ were happy to be in line for a hand out from TARP to protect their own wealth when the dominoes started

Poverty, Politics and Race
(The View From Down Here)

to fall from their bad decisions. Yet, they resented the President's weatherization stimulus program that repaired old heating and cooling units, replaced windows and doors, and properly insulated old homes for elderly, disabled, and poor households.

These homes, without such energy efficiency measures, would be dangerously cold in winter and hot enough in summers _ particularly in the South_ to present major health concerns for the elderly and children. Also, the construction industry, without the jobs the program created, would have added thousands more to the unemployment and food stamp lines due to almost certain layoffs instead of the recovery under President Obama.

The U.S. Census Bureau reported in 2011 that the U.S. poverty rate had risen to 15.1%. Children living in single female headed households had a poverty rate of 47.1% compared to 8.3% for two parent households and 19.6% for single male headed households. The average income of those with less than a 9th grade education was $20,805 based on 2007 federal statistics compared to over $40,000 for high school graduates; and up to $100,000 for those with a professional degree. The largest age group living in poverty is made up of children under the age of 18. These statistics show that under educated, single female-headed households with children are more likely to be poor.

Education, as my parents insisted during my childhood, is still an important doorway out of poverty and gives support to President Obama's

Poverty, Politics and Race
(The View From Down Here)

commitment to increased funding for Pell Grants and public education. However, poverty among female-headed, single parent households is not a mandate for more marriage initiatives; but rather demonstrates the wisdom and importance of the Lilly Ledbetter Act, requiring equal pay for women, in lifting women and their children out of poverty.

Often only the percentage of each ethnic population living in poverty is reported in studies, making it easy for people like Newt Gingrich, Santorum, and Ryan to misrepresent the true face of poverty. Mostly Republican politicians have created a stereotype of the poor that is Black, lazy, unemployed, involved in illegal activity, and happy to live off the kindness of all other hard working Americans. And, if I only quoted the poverty rates, without including the actual number of people living in poverty by ethnicity or race, those politicians might find a way to continue presenting that false image of the poor.

However, I don't plan to leave them that opening.

There were 223.6 million White Americans in the U.S. based on the 2010 census. The White poverty rate was 9.9%, which seems low until informed that the White poverty rate equates to 22.1 million White Americans living at or below the federal poverty level. White children make up 57% of children in poverty in rural communities.

There were 38.9 million Black Americans, with a poverty rate of 27.4% or 10.7 million Blacks at the poverty level. The Hispanic population was

Poverty, Politics and Race
(The View From Down Here)

50.5 million, with a poverty rate of 26.6%, for a total of 13.4 million Hispanics at the federal poverty level. Asians made up 14.7 million of the U.S. population, with a poverty rate of 12.1%, or 1.8 million at the federal poverty level.

These figures make it clear that the GOP will need to develop a new profile for the average American in poverty with 22.1 million White Americans living in poverty compared to 10.7 million Black Americans and 13.4 million Hispanics. But if the purpose for using the tried and true stereotypes is to throw raw meat to the racist element in their base of support, the facts probably won't matter.

The chart shows the maximum income, based on number of persons in the household, in order to qualify for most of the federal safety net programs to assist Americans experiencing major financial hardships. And a single person or two person household, at the maximum annual income on the chart for the number in the household, would only have a monthly income of $916 and $1250 respectively for housing, food, utilities and fuel oil costs, with little if anything left for transportation.

Poverty, Politics and Race (The View From Down Here)

Number of Persons in Household	Maximum Annual Income to meet Poverty Guidelines in 48 states and D.C.	Maximum Income in Alaska	Maximum Income in Hawaii
1	$11,170	$13,970	$12,860
2	$15,130	$18,920	$17,410
3	$19,090	$23,870	$21,960
4	$23,050	$28,820	$26,510
5	$27,010	$33,770	$31,060
6	$30,970	$38,720	$35,610
7	$34,930	$43,670	$40,160
8	$38,890	$48,620	$44,710
For each additional person in household add:	$3,960	$4,950	$4,550

{*2011 – 2012 Federal Poverty Guidelines}

Based on the chart, a family of four with an annual income of $23,050 would have a monthly income of just $1,921.00, barely enough for rent, food, and utilities, and some transportation cost. Heaven help them if there are emergency medical, car repair expenses, or the utility bill peaks during a very hot summer or equally cold winter. Any increase in monthly expenses would throw the family into financial chaos. Further, in many cases, these families are working more than one low paying job to cobble together an income of $1,920 monthly.

Poverty, Politics and Race (The View From Down Here)

It also depends on where the poor live whether their circumstances are made even worse. In rural communities with few resources and very limited job options for both the educated and under-educated, residents often must travel 50 to 100 miles round trip daily for employment. With the cost of gas and no form of low cost public transportation for the poor who usually do not own cars, the transportation costs require a higher percentage of the budget and make it difficult to stretch the pay check for housing, food, and utility costs.

Some of these small rural towns do not even have grocery stores or hospitals, requiring long distance travel costs to buy groceries or take care of a medical emergency. The local Seven Eleven Stores are the major option for those without transportation, requiring much higher prices for very limited and less nutritious food choices.

Small towns in which tourism is the primary industry provide many low paying service jobs in hotels, restaurants, and shops. However, the high priced vacation homes of the non-residents on whom the economy depends drive up the rental and home ownership rates for residents; making housing unaffordable for most of those with low and modest incomes. Priced out of the housing market, many must live farther and farther away from their place of employment, creating a drain on their already poverty or near poverty level wages for travel and childcare costs.

Even in urban environments, such a large portion of earnings by the working poor must be used for transportation or childcare at hours and days in

Poverty, Politics and Race (The View From Down Here)

which both are most difficult to find and afford, that they still find it hard to pay rent, utilities, and put food on the table. For housing to be affordable, the cost should not exceed 33% of the monthly income.

A single parent with 2 children earning $1600 monthly would be over-income, based on the federal poverty guidelines, in every state except Alaska and Hawaii, to receive rental assistance through most of the safety net programs. An affordable rent for this household would be $528 monthly. It is difficult if not impossible in many communities to find safe, habitable housing at that rate. Even worse, the working poor earn much less on average and are left raising their children in the most deplorable conditions imaginable.

Ex-offenders are often released from prison and sent back into communities with little education, job training, or resources and immediately become among the community's poor and homeless population. With criminal records, even in a good economy, they face added complications and barriers. Even with workforce development offices providing bonds to protect employers from risks involved in hiring ex-offenders, few hire from this population. Further, many property managers and rental agents prohibit leasing to ex-offenders, even if they have stable income to maintain the housing.

When non-violent ex-offenders return to their communities and are locked out of opportunities for jobs, housing, and often are denied reunification with their children, they are left with few options except recidivism. Added to that, states like Florida make it almost impossible for ex-offenders to have their rights restored. Florida's Republican Governor Rick Scott,

Poverty, Politics and Race (The View From Down Here)

elected in 2010, set to work immediately upon taking his oath ridding the state of former Governor Crist's more progressive and fair restoration of rights laws and guidelines.

The Governor and his Republican controlled Legislature, also, required ultra sounds for women considering an abortion, state mandated drug testing for TANF, Food Stamp, or Medicaid applicants at the cash strapped client's expense. They passed voter suppression laws that impacted more directly minorities, poor, and young voters, along with the total climination of the more progressive restoration of rights process for ex-offenders.

With the state providing almost no funding for re-entry programs to smooth the successful reintegration of ex-offenders into the community, the state almost guaranteed higher recidivism rates. Maybe that's Governor Scott's plan. By making sure the prisons stay full, he ensures the private prison management industry_ that became a cottage industry under a Republican state legislature_ continues to prosper at the expense of the public and the poor. Jobs created through prevention, rehabilitation, and re-entry programs are far preferable and more beneficial to the community, families, and the ex-offenders than repeat incarceration.

The biggest problem with putting a real human face on poverty, though, is that too often we get caught up in the statistics and the people get lost in the numbers. That's why I have chosen to end this chapter with two real life stories that best illustrate how difficult it can be for even well meaning people to

Poverty, Politics and Race (The View From Down Here)

really understand the devastating circumstances of those living in poverty in our country.

It would really be an eye opener if Obama administration officials and Congressional leaders would take a tour with local faith-based and non-profit leaders of poverty stricken areas in their communities. They would see firsthand the conditions in which many Americans live. They would not soon forget the experience.

A good example is the middle-aged woman who approached me at the conclusion of a community meeting. She desperately needed help and had already exhausted other options. She had been living for many years in a very old, single wide, mobile home. The condition of the home had deteriorated such that ceiling tiles were molded and falling down, and the floors had rotted out completely in certain rooms. Large rodents were coming into the house through the holes in the floor that opened to the ground below. Afraid to stay in the house, she had begun sleeping in her old car in the yard.

At the time, I was executive director of a community action agency and agreed to meet her at her home in a neighboring county the next day for a site visit. Upon arrival, I was appalled at the dilapidated condition of the home, and that no one had helped her. With her permission, I was able to bring her desperate plight to the attention of the local media, governmental, faith-based, and business leaders, while mobilizing resources within our agency to provide emergency assistance and case management. As a result, her application for a home through the county's Community Development Block Grant program was

Poverty, Politics and Race (The View From Down Here)

given top priority. Community donations provided the needed resources for her temporary relocation, as well as the purchase of household goods for her new, affordable home when completed.

If not for her determination, she like thousands of other Americans would have been forced to continue living in unsafe and uninhabitable conditions. The greatest shame, though, is that most of those left in these deplorable circumstances are children and low-income elderly.

Really poor Americans have affordable housing options that are safe and livable. The poor often live in housing that is old, in need of major repair, insulation, and an efficiency overhaul.

Poverty, Politics and Race (The View From Down Here)

And finally, my first year as a resident of North Florida and a young wife and mother of a two year old, I accepted a teaching position in a rural community about 40 miles from Tallahassee – my family's place of residence. The school was new and modern, replacing the old, small wooden structure that had served the community's children for as long as most residents could remember. This was the only elementary school that served children of the town's leaders and the children of the poorest residents. It was easy to see the disparity in the children's circumstances. One first grader I'll call Michael for the sake of using a name not his given name caught everyone's attention almost immediately.

Each day Michael came to school in dirty ragged clothing and his class mates refused to sit near him; teasing him about body odor. A note was sent home by Michael's homeroom teacher notifying the parent(s) that the school expected Michael to be sent to school clean and in clean clothing each day. When Michael continued to come to school in a disheveled state, the principal called together an intervention team made up of all of Michael's teachers, the guidance counselor, school social worker, and Sheriff's department resource officer to determine if this was a case of child neglect; and if so, the steps required to address the problem. In the meantime, both the homeroom teacher and guidance counselor had worked with Michael's class to stop the teasing and bullying. The new school was built with a shower in the restroom adjoining the school clinic. Each morning before school started, Michael was allowed to shower and change into new clothing teachers had pooled funds to purchase for him.

Poverty, Politics and Race (The View From Down Here)

Yet, some teachers had begun asking, "What kind of parents would allow a child to leave home in that condition?" Within weeks, the intervention team decided that a school team should do a home visit to determine the living conditions in the home, before making a child neglect report to the Florida Department of Children and Families. The team included the Guidance Counselor, the school social worker, the resource officer, and me.

Upon arriving at the home - a barely standing two-room shack isolated miles from the school on a two-lane rural roadway a lot became immediately clear. Stepping inside, and almost falling through missing floor boards, we greeted Michael's mother who had a small child in her arms and one holding on to her leg, I saw the wood stove and that the house had no running water. We talked and learned they were share croppers on the tobacco farm and owned almost nothing.

As I was poised to ask about Michael, I saw him walking across the field straining to carry a bucket of water that had to weigh almost as much as he did. The officer rushed to help him. There was no longer any question why this child came to school unbathed most days. When the only source of water is a spigot in the middle of a field where this small child must cross a street and walk a great distance for a bucket of water, that water becomes a precious commodity for cooking, cleaning dishes, and drinking. There is likely none left to regularly wash clothes or even bathe.

Obviously in a very impoverished circumstance, the mother was under great stress trying to take care of her young children, and little Michael had

Poverty, Politics and Race (The View From Down Here)

responsibilities at home far beyond his young age. Our hearts went out to this young family and we vowed to immediately launch a campaign for them in town to create a safer, more stable home environment. The community came together to provide for the crisis needs of the family and the mother was warned that it was dangerous for a child as young as Michael to cross the street; and further walking that far carrying a heavy bucket of water was harmful to his health. The family was asked to make arrangements to schedule that task when one of the adults could go for the water. The school team went to work developing a plan to address the family's needs comprehensively. A state case worker was assigned to make sure the family received help with basic needs and to monitor the children in the household.

A couple of years later after I had found a teaching position in Tallahassee, I received the horrible news. I will never forget the day we were notified that Michael had been hit by a car as he crossed the street with the buckets of water for his family. Though he was taken by life flight to the closest hospital trauma center in Tallahassee, Michael died from his injuries. Michael's short life, filled with hardship, is a very sad memory that will stay with me the rest of my life.

And I will also remember the promise he never lived to fulfill. It is a reminder that those impacted most by poverty are our nation's children. They are the most vulnerable and have the least control over their circumstances.

Those who know him best may be right that Mitt Romney is a good and decent man. But the Mitt

Poverty, Politics and Race (The View From Down Here)

Romney, who believed that the poor do not deserve his concern, or even healthcare, food or housing, just did not get it. And for that reason, was not ready and did not deserve to lead this country now or in the future.

Chapter 3

The Rules Are Different For Minorities and the Poor

Poverty, Politics and Race (The View From Down Here)

The overblown controversy over the Association of Community Organizations for Reform Now (ACORN) and the speed with which Congress voted to shut it down were breathtaking. Particularly so, since the federal government and ACORN's right wing accusers have shown a curious blindness to actual fraud and waste of federal funds by large corporations like Halliburton's Kellogg Brown & Root (KBR), as compared to the absence of evidence of such documented acts by ACORN. Yet, this national organization was tried in the media, then convicted and sentenced by Congress with no semblance of a fair and objective hearing.

America has always had a different set of rules for the rich and powerful than for the rest of us. It has just become so much worse over the last decade. First, the federal government requires a very strict bid and procurement process for non-profits and public sector entities that receive federal funds. The policies generally require competitive bid procedures to purchase goods and services in amounts of $5000 and above. Yet federal agencies like the Pentagon are not required to follow the government's own rules even when dealing with multi-million dollar contracts. This is a clear case of a "do as I say, not as I do" policy for certain governmental agencies.

While placing huge restrictions and monitoring requirements on community-based organizations receiving relatively small grants, Congress has been silent for years as multi-billion dollar, **no-bid** contracts have been awarded by the military to KBR and other wealthy corporations with friends in high places. A simple comparison of the government's differing

Poverty, Politics and Race (The View From Down Here)

response to KBR and the ACORN case illustrates this point perfectly.

ACORN, a non-partisan, non-profit founded in 1970 with a mission to empower low income residents and communities through jobs, access to affordable housing, and increased voter registration, has had a target on its back by the Right for a very long time. In recent years, the GOP added ACORN to its enemies list after noting the success of the organization in registering voters who usually voted Democratic. Regularly, Republicans challenged ACORN's right to receive public funding and sought opportunities to bring the organization down.

They got their chance in 2009 when workers in three different ACORN offices were caught making questionable comments and engaged in equally questionable behavior on a hidden camera sting set up by GOP operatives. The video, edited to create a much more harmful version of the actual interaction with ACORN staff, was immediately released to national news organizations and on the internet, creating a public relations nightmare for ACORN nationwide.

With the speed of light, Congress convened and voted to withdraw the existing funding and any hope of future funding for all ACORN offices in the nation; though only three offices were involved in the sting. I cannot remember any other time in recent history that Congress has acted as swiftly, and with as little factual information. Even when the nation's economy was crumbling in late 2008, Congress did not act as swiftly to investigate the financial institutions that almost destroyed our economy as it did on the ACORN defunding.

Poverty, Politics and Race (The View From Down Here)

It seemed unusually harsh, since ACORN, nor its employees, was never charged or found guilty of any fraud, criminal wrongdoing, or misuse of federal funds in either of these cases. ACORN's crime was that a handful of staff from three of its offices were tricked into making stupid, indefensible statements captured on camera. There was no evidence presented that these employees actually violated any program guidelines or were guilty of misuse of federal funds.

Further, those harmed most by withdrawing all federal funds were the poorest and most vulnerable Americans, who desperately needed the services from the organization.

ACORN had received $53 million nationwide for its offices from 1994-2009; crumbs when compared to the waste and fraud by large corporations like KBR in which evidence of fraud and misuse of federal funds was plentiful. Yet KBR continues as a major federal contractor to this date.

Compare the ACORN case to KBR's no-bid $25 billion contract since 2001 with the U.S. Armed Services. The purpose of the KBR contract was to build and maintain military bases in Iraq, feed, house, and provide transportation for the troops. There were two unusual features about the contract. First, it was a no-bid contract for such an enormous purchase of goods and services, though there were other companies interested and capable of competing for the contract.

Therefore, it would be hard for the government to make the case that KBR was a sole source vendor. Second, it was a "cost-plus" contract which allowed KBR to receive a 1% share of the cost for every

Poverty, Politics and Race (The View From Down Here)

purchase – removing any incentive to hold down costs or seek deals for the tax payers. The higher the cost for the purchase, the more money the 1% incentive generated for the company. They were even eligible for an additional 2% on each purchase if KBR operated in an efficient and honest manner.

Based on what standard? Evidence shows massive waste and overcharges with no consequences and a free flow of incentive pay to the contractors in spite of their questionable performance. So there was obviously no real oversight and monitoring to determine the quality of the contractor's performance. Yet the government continued to hand out the bonus checks.

And here's the most mind blowing, tragic part of this story. In January 2008, a young American serving in Iraq was electrocuted while in the shower built by KBR. The electrocution was attributed to KBR's poor electrical work. There were eighteen electrocutions attributed to poor safety standards by KBR, due to faulty wiring and improper grounding since 2003, according to federal reports.

A special CNN investigative report stated, "The Pentagon's Defense Contract Management Agency gave KBR a level III Corrective Action Request, issued when a contractor is found in 'serious non-compliance', just one step below the possibility of suspending or terminating a contract, a Pentagon official said."

What?!?!?! The faulty, negligent work of Halliburton's KBR caused the death of maybe 18 of our soldiers serving their country overseas, and they only received a disciplinary report from the U.S.

Poverty, Politics and Race (The View From Down Here)

government, while ACORN had its funding terminated for the acts of poor judgment that harmed no one except ACORN. Even more egregious – KBR was awarded another $35 billion contract by the Pentagon after the electrocutions became known. Where was Congress's swift enforcement and even-handed justice in this case? After all, nothing ACORN did caused the loss of life or property. The same cannot be said for KBR.

It is not hard to see the discrepancy and unequal treatment. But, why? A hint might be the fact that the U.S. Vice President at the time, Dick Cheney, was a former CEO of Halliburton, KBR's parent company. That's power and influence. The biggest beneficiaries of ACORN's work and resources were the poor. And the poor have little power, and were no match for highly paid, powerful lobbyists of wealthy corporations like Halliburton, in demanding the attention of the Bush Administration or Congress on their issues.

And, likewise, in the case of Dr. Henry Louis Gates, the narrative was clearly and unfairly skewered in favor of the White police officer involved and against the renowned Harvard professor. Records show Dr. Gates, a noted author, internationally known Harvard professor and researcher who also happened to be Black, upon returning home from a China trip found the door lock at his Cambridge home jammed. As he and his driver worked to get the door open, a neighbor noticed and was concerned there might be a break-in in progress and called the police department.

By the time officers arrived, Dr. Gates had been successful getting into his home. When confronted by

Poverty, Politics and Race (The View From Down Here)

Sgt. Crowley, a White officer in the Cambridge Police Department, Professor Gates readily produced both his driver's license and Harvard University faculty identification to prove he was indeed the homeowner and not a burglar. From that point forward, we only know each man's version of what happened next. We do know the result. Dr. Gates was arrested and taken to jail on a disorderly conduct charge by Sgt. Crowley.

Crowley reported that the professor "exhibited loud and tumultuous behavior" when confronted and accused him of racism. By the time the arrest took place, the officer had already confirmed there was no break in and the person standing before him was the legal homeowner. Why didn't Crowley simply apologize to the professor for the inconvenience, after it was clear there was no crime in progress and leave, instead of escalating the situation by making the professor feel he was still under suspicion? Most White people would not understand Professor Gates' anger at being treated and spoken to like a criminal in his own home. It's understandable. They have not had to contain their anger at being under estimated, disrespected, and treated like second class citizens most of their lives, regardless of their hard work, and accomplishments.

The news media thought it was incredulous that anyone considered race a factor in Dr. Gates' arrest. Blacks, however, found it just as incredulous that the mostly White news media did not see the obvious racism involved in the escalation of this situation, which could have easily ended differently. After all, in repeated news stories, Crowley's skill at conducting sensitivity, diversity, and racial profiling workshops was pointed to as proof that he could not possibly have caused the problem.

Poverty, Politics and Race (The View From Down Here)

Yet nothing about Dr. Gates' long, distinguished career and accomplishments caused them to give him the same benefit of the doubt, as they eagerly assigned blame for his arrest only to him. The same media would have been hard pressed, however, to find Black Americans who believed that Crowley would have treated a White homeowner in the same circumstance in the disrespectful manner in which Gates was treated. Likewise, most_ including me_ would have felt just as offended by Crowley's behavior.

The disorderly conduct charge was later dropped. I believe there never would have been one had Gates been White. A different rule would have been applied.

While middle America, minorities, and the poor are at the mercy of those we elect to ensure our rights are protected, until Congress develops the courage to level the playing field between the rich, powerful few, and low to middle income Americans and we are honest in admitting racism still exists, this kind of injustice will continue to be a major embarrassment for a country that claims "all men are created equal".

The disparity in the way ACORN was treated by Congress, and the continued coddling of wealthy corporate raiders like Halliburton and KBR, and the Wall Street crowd, are the clearest examples I can give that we don't always get the government we deserve. We, instead, get the government the wealthiest and most influential Americans can buy.

Congressman Paul Ryan, later Governor Mitt Romney's vice presidential running mate, authored a U.S. House Budget that would continue to feed the

Poverty, Politics and Race (The View From Down Here)

gluttony of the Pentagon, reward the greed of the wealthy with an added 10% tax cut beyond the already low Bush rate, while sacrificing food, housing, college tuition, unemployment benefits, jobs, healthcare, and childcare subsidies for the poor. By taking from the poor to give to the rich, he was lauded by his colleagues and the media as smart and courageous. At the same time, many in the media saw no irony in Ryan coming up with money in the budget to continue subsidies for oil companies that were drowning in unprecedented profits while children were going to bed hungry and homeless due to home foreclosures and joblessness caused by the deep recession during the Bush administration.

Maybe heartless would be a better description than courageous for Mr. Ryan. It took no courage to launch an assault on the most vulnerable among us while ingratiating himself to the powerful and rich like himself. And while he, as a U.S. Congressman, enjoyed the best healthcare plan our tax dollars could buy, he cared little about the impact of his recommendation to savage Medicaid for the poor, Medicare for the elderly, and the Affordable Healthcare Act for almost 50 million uninsured middle income Americans.

These inequities have created an America almost unrecognizable as the democracy envisioned in our Constitution. It is a shameful statement about who we are as a country. It will be an even greater shame if those of us who disagree accept this as our future instead of taking action to create the kind of America that allows all Americans the opportunity to thrive and succeed. The power the rest of us have is not in dollars, but our vote. When we stop bowing to the interests of those already too firmly and comfortably

Poverty, Politics and Race (The View From Down Here)

established in the seats of power, and start voting our own collective interests, we will reclaim our power and correct these inequities.

Poverty, Politics and Race (The View From Down Here)

Chapter 4

The Role of Government

Poverty, Politics and Race (The View From Down Here)

When commenting on presidential candidate Mitt Romney's gaffe, "I'm not concerned about the very poor", Joe Scarborough on Morning Joe opined that if Mitt had explained how many people the free market had lifted out of poverty, compared to the safety net, Romney would have been fine. Joe made it an either- or proposition; and in doing so, displayed his lack of understanding of the challenges of the poor and poverty in America.

Newt Gingrich noted the poor needed a trampoline, not a safety net. But the poor can't just propel themselves out of poverty no matter how great the market performs. It takes time. It takes helping hands. It takes a safety net of support until they can stand confidently on their own feet.

The poor need assistance with education, job skills, job placement, and actual jobs to create stable income and stand on their own two feet. The federal safety net programs are necessary components of any plan to help the poor transition from financial crisis to financial independence, as recognized by the Clinton, Bush, and Obama administrations.

The multi-tiered Temporary Assistance to Needy Families (TANF) program requires recipients to actively seek education, job training, and employment, as a condition of receiving public assistance. In spite of false 2012 Romney campaign ads that President Obama acted to eliminate work requirements of the TANF Program, the state waivers approved by the President only allowed the states flexibility in the design and implementation

Poverty, Politics and Race (The View From Down Here)

of the work requirement, as requested by Governors; including Republican governors.

The federal safety net gives the poor the means to stabilize their immediate financial crisis, and then, provides the resources, referrals and support to help them develop the employability and job skills necessary to make the leap from the trampoline into the free market jobs successfully. It is difficult to impossible to move up the ladder from abject poverty to middle income overnight. Without the return of some of each state's federal tax dollars to support the overwhelming needs of their residents, a much heavier burden would be placed on state and local governments to raise more revenues through higher taxes.

Ryan and his Republican colleagues in the U.S. House of Representatives are very fond of pointing out that the federal government must have a balanced budget like states are required to maintain. They, however, never mention that when states must overspend to meet the most urgent needs of residents and the government, they have simply raided state trust funds and eliminated services to the most needy in order to plug deficit holes in their budgets. Further, these states continue large corporate tax breaks, drastically reducing state revenues, while at the same time they have avoided their responsibility by passing unfunded mandates down to local governments and local tax payers.

Many of these same lawmakers are fond of saying that the federal safety net programs only

Poverty, Politics and Race (The View From Down Here)

make the poor dependent on government, rather than giving them a path to self sufficiency. Wisconsin Congressman Paul Ryan said, "We don't want to turn the safety net into a hammock". Minnesota Congresswoman Michelle Bachman famously said, "Those who will not work should not eat". However, she was silent on how she would distinguish between those unwilling to work and the millions of Americans without jobs through no fault of their own. Nor did she address her planned starvation of poor children. Or was she planning to change the child labor laws so that children can "work for food"?

Statements like those only demonstrate how out of touch they are with their own federal programs. All of these programs are designed to create a bridge from poverty to financial independence and a more successful future. And certainly there is recognition that some resources are necessary for crisis services while the poor work their way up the ladder from extreme crisis to stability and financial independence.

Prime examples are the Community Services Block Grant (CSBG), Pell Grants, Temporary Assistance to Needy Families (TANF), Earned Income Tax Credit (EITC), Childcare and Development Fund, and Head Start. Many of these elected officials probably need to spend a little more time learning about the government programs they regularly rail against. In an effort to enlighten, here are insights into some of the more prominent anti-poverty bridge programs currently funded by the federal government.

Poverty, Politics and Race (The View From Down Here)

In addition to the programs already mentioned, the U.S. Department of Housing and Urban Development (HUD) Housing Vouchers, Supplemental Nutrition Assistance Program (SNAP or Food Stamps), Supplemental Nutrition Program for Women, Infants, and Children (WIC), Medicaid, Medicare Part D, State Child Health Insurance Program, Free or Reduced-price school Breakfast and Lunch, Childcare and Development Fund, and the Low Income Home Energy Assistance Program (LIHEAP) are necessary to stabilizing the household. Once the crisis subsides, families are better able to focus on creating a Financial Independence Plan, with clear and realistic education, job training, and career goals.

The following is a brief description of some of the most prominent safety net programs.

Housing Vouchers through HUD subsidizes the rent of residents with incomes at or below 55% of area median income (AMI), for up to 70% of the rent. This makes housing affordable and accessible to the poor who are working to improve their financial circumstances.

Temporary Assistance to Needy Families (TANF) is monthly cash assistance for families with children, with benefits limited by the federal government to no more than five (5) years. States may lower or increase the five year time limit. The federal law requires recipients to work or to be enrolled in school to demonstrate their responsibility and commitment to work to improve their own circumstances, instead of long-term

Poverty, Politics and Race (The View From Down Here)

dependency on these programs. Though the GOP falsely claimed that the President's approval of waivers requested by states eliminated the work requirement, these waivers are nothing new, keep work requirements intact, and are commonly requested by both Republican and Democratic governors to allow flexibility in the design of their programs for better outcomes.

The **Supplemental Nutrition Assistance Program (SNAP)**, or Food Stamps, is financial assistance in the form of a paper voucher or debit card that allows the poor, who meet income eligibility requirements, the means to purchase food for their families. For example, a family of 4, with an income of no more than $2,422 per month, would be eligible for Food Stamps. Many of these families, forced by circumstances into minimum wage, often part-time jobs without benefits, earn much less than the $2422 cited; and generally the month lasts a lot longer than the money to pay for basic needs for the household. Most of us could not imagine how to stretch $900 to $1200 a month to cover rent, utilities, food, transportation, and childcare expenses. It often is very difficult "to make ends meet", as my Mother used to say, even with federal assistance.

The **Women, Infants, and Children** (WIC) or Special Supplemental Nutrition Program is a food, healthcare, and nutrition education program for pregnant women and mothers with children 5 years old and younger. To be eligible, a household of 4 cannot earn more than $3,446 monthly. It ensures that the most vulnerable poor population, children,

Poverty, Politics and Race (The View From Down Here)

are nourished and healthy, and that mothers receive prenatal care to ensure healthy infants and prevent infant mortality. The program not only helps these poor families, but provides real savings for the public in avoided chronic healthcare costs.

Medicaid provides access to health services for low-income elderly, people with disabilities, and dependent children and poor families. **Medicare Part D** provides discounted prescriptions drugs for seniors. Without this assistance, emergency rooms would be overrun, and the poor would receive healthcare only in crisis when there are fewer treatment options and the care is the most expensive. These programs allow for preventive and timely attention to health needs of the poor at a more affordable cost to the patient and the public.

State Children's Health Insurance Program (SCHIP) provides discounted healthcare services for poor children who are not eligible for Medicaid, in homes in which parents cannot afford healthcare coverage. These are often families who are employed but with no employer provided health coverage. The Affordable Healthcare Act will ensure millions more Americans access to healthcare coverage when it takes full effect in 2014.

The **Free School Breakfast and Lunch Program** ensures that school children in households with incomes no more than $3,446 monthly, with a family of 4, receive two nutritious meals each school day to prevent hunger, and allow them to concentrate and do their best in school. Hungry

Poverty, Politics and Race (The View From Down Here)

children find it hard to focus in school when their most basic needs are not met.

The **Earned Income Tax Credit** is a credit against federal taxes for the working poor earning very low wages. The maximum credit or refund for a household with 3 or more children is $5,751. These households were among the Americans with whom the GOP had concerns that they paid no taxes, while justifying their position on no tax increase for the wealthiest 2% of Americans. It is incredible to me that the GOP sees no irony in demanding the elimination of this credit to stabilize the financial conditions of the poor, while steadfast and stubbornly insisting on cutting taxes another 10% for wealthy Americans and continuing oil subsidies for wealthy oil companies. I think that's called "corporate welfare". You can almost hear Scrooge saying, in response to the request for a donation for the poor in the Charles Dickens' classic **A Christmas Carol**, "Are there no work houses?"

The **Childcare and Development Fund** provides free or reduced-cost childcare to help working poor parents of infant, preschool, and school-age children to improve their opportunities for employment or higher paying jobs to overcome poverty. Without this benefit, the working poor's options would be to (1) spend almost all of their earnings on childcare, (2) leave children unattended or in less safe, less nurturing environments; or (3) remain dependent on government by not working. None of these are good choices. The childcare subsidy frees the parent to work while ensuring a

Poverty, Politics and Race (The View From Down Here)

safe and nurturing environment for their young children.

Supplemental Security Income is cash assistance to poor seniors and people with disabilities. It would surprise most Americans to learn that these monthly checks, some as low as $674, would not even cover the rent if not for assistance available through other safety net programs. Based on HUD guidelines, housing is affordable if the cost is no more than 30 to 33% of the household income. A senior living alone with a $674 to $1000 social security check as the only source of income, and a monthly rent of $400 to $600, clearly does not meet that HUD standard for housing affordability.

Unfortunately, based on market rental rates in most communities, many poor Americans who do not have the benefit of subsidized housing end up with housing costs exceeding 50% of their monthly income. And with the high demand for housing assistance, many low-income residents find themselves on waiting lists for years as they struggle to keep their heads above water. Further, in many of these cases age, disability, and poor health made it impossible to work to supplement very low monthly incomes.

Pell Grants provide financial assistance and access to college education for children of middle and low-income households. Though there is no low-income eligibility requirement, the poorest students receive the largest grants. With the rapid escalation over the past decade in college costs, a

Poverty, Politics and Race (The View From Down Here)

college education would be completely out of reach for the majority of American students without the access these grants and federally backed student loans provide. A good education remains an important gateway to jobs and better pay.

Head Start, one of the historic anti-poverty programs from the 1960s, provides a comprehensive school readiness program for low-income three and four year old preschoolers, including meals, dental, health, speech therapy, and developmental screenings to ensure that children enrolled in the program will start kindergarten prepared to compete on a level playing field with children from homes of greater means. **Early Head Start** extended these important early childhood development services to low-income children birth to 3 years old. A more detailed report on the Head Start Program is covered in chapter 11.

The **Low-Income Home Energy Assistance Program** (LIHEAP), provides assistance with heating and cooling expenses, utility and fuel bills for low-income households. Priority is given to low-income households of the elderly, disabled, and families with young children. This program not only provides much needed assistance to low-income families, but also is a major benefit to utility providers by paying customer bills that otherwise would be uncollectible accounts on their bottom line. As a result, non-profits and governmental agencies that manage these programs have ready allies in their community's utility providers who benefit as much as the low income residents from the LIHEAP program.

Poverty, Politics and Race (The View From Down Here)

The **Weatherization Assistance Program (WAP)** provides energy efficiency improvements to homes of low-income Americans to lower utility consumption and bills. This not only benefits the low-income recipients, but delays the need for new energy generation by local governments and private utility providers. Further, it creates private sector jobs in the construction industry, allowing these contractors to hire new workers and retain existing employees through these funds to retrofit homes for greater energy efficiency. WAP projects are of particular benefit to small contractors in retaining jobs in the large cities and small towns where the work is being done.

Most of these program funds are administered through state agencies that contract with provider agencies or local governments for the direct delivery of these services throughout the United States. This gives a further boost to these local economies.

Congressman Paul Ryan's 2012 Budget for the U.S. House of Representatives, **The Path to Prosperity – Restoring America's Promise**, speaks of the need for "policies aimed at helping the less fortunate get back on their feet while encouraging the chronically impoverished to achieve greater control over their lives." His recommendations for the drastic reduction or elimination of many of the safety net and bridge programs that lead to self sufficiency, however, would do the exact opposite. The problem is not that there is too much funding for these programs. The safety net programs make up a relatively small percentage of the federal

Poverty, Politics and Race (The View From Down Here)

budget. The problem is too little investment to address the multiple, complex needs of the poor so that more than a small fraction of impoverished Americans and poor communities can move up the ladder to self sufficiency.

For a country with 15.1% of all Americans living in poverty in 2012, the highest poverty rate since 1983 according to the National Poverty Center, the maximum federal annual appropriation for the Community Services Block Grant (CSBG) has been approximately $600,000,000. Florida, the fourth highest populated state in the U.S. after California, New York, and Texas, received a total 2011 block grant of $19.5 million to assist over 2,000,000 residents living at or below the federal poverty guideline with the resources and skills to make the transition from desperate poverty to financial independence.

In President Obama's 2012 budget proposal, the CSBG federal grant was being proposed for a cut of close to 50%, which seems contrary to achieving the program's goals. And, if approved by Congress, the President's recommendation would result in the elimination of some of the programs in Florida's smaller, rural counties, with annual allocations as low as $25,000. Even if the full allocation was dedicated to direct client services at $2500 per household annually, it would only allow 10 of the hundreds of poor residents in these towns to receive help with childcare, transportation, GED, on the job training, and jobs, even if the programs excluded the emergency component for rental or

Poverty, Politics and Race (The View From Down Here)

mortgage assistance, food, prescription vouchers, and utility deposits.

None of these small counties have public transportation available. Therefore, gas vouchers or by-the-trip private van transportation to school or jobs located in the county seat, for rural counties with several towns scattered miles apart throughout the county, could easily deplete the $2500 allocation long before the end of a year. Further, there would be nothing left for emergency assistance with food, rent, or childcare to address immediate needs to allow the client's complete focus on improving financial circumstances.

The governmental and non-profit agencies charged with coordinating these programs, with so little funding, are given an almost impossible job. In reality, the recession-driven need created such a high demand for service, at a time when funding was being reduced to little more than $400 per client annually, that the rate of poverty continued to grow. The funding levels do not even begin to cover the complex services necessary to take a low-income resident or household from crisis and extreme poverty to self sufficiency.

Under such circumstances, it seems a bit unfair to expect these community agencies to perform miracles with so little support to get the job done. It is through the dedication of sorely underpaid, but hard working Case Managers that the necessary guidance, coaching, and mentoring for each client is provided, while also serving as the client's best advocate.

Poverty, Politics and Race (The View From Down Here)

As a former executive director of a community action agency serving 8 North Florida counties, all very different with their own special challenges, collaboration and partnership skills were a must in developing the resources to achieve program goals and meet local match requirements of these federal programs. Excellent partnerships with local governments, school districts, colleges, universities, vocational schools, chambers of commerce, workforce development boards, local employers, banks, community-based health centers, housing agencies, faith-based organizations, and other human service agencies leveraged hundreds of thousands in non-federal in-kind and cash match on the agency's federal grant programs.

For that North Florida community action agency, the Community Services Block Grant allocation was only about $500,000 for 8 counties, with a combined poverty population of close to 80,000. That's about $6.25 annually per person meeting the poverty income guideline for services in those 8 counties.

How could Congress or the President realistically expect poverty to be eradicated or even meaningfully impacted on such a starvation budget? So for those folks who regularly ask the question, why is there still so much poverty even with the millions spent by the federal government each year, the answer is simple. Six dollars will hardly buy a loaf of bread and a jar of peanut butter. It buys almost nothing toward reversing years of poverty and deprivation for a full year.

Poverty, Politics and Race (The View From Down Here)

Further, many years of a bad economy increased the number of people in poverty. Congress could not possibly think that, with an economic meltdown at the end of 2008 that resulted in almost 800,000 Americans losing jobs monthly, there would be no increase in the poverty rate or the number of people needing food stamps or other safety net programs. There is a clear cause and effect relationship here that even a blind person would be able to see.

Without the partnerships, the many innovative projects and services like the agency's micro-business training and loan program that allowed low-income people to create income by starting their own businesses and self employment, would not have been possible. And neither would the creation of the first weatherization installer certification class in the nation, with its community college and workforce development partners, have been available to prepare low-income participants with skills for the weatherization jobs created by federal stimulus. Wise targeting of very limited funds made it possible to train low-income participants for jobs in areas in which jobs actually existed, such as in health related occupations.

Nationally accredited, high quality Head Start centers ensured that the most vulnerable_ poor children_ received a good start toward a successful future by preparing them to enter school with the requisite skills to perform at the correct age and developmental level. None of these services would be possible, even for the small fraction of the poor who benefit, if not for the necessary federal

Poverty, Politics and Race (The View From Down Here)

safety net. It is just not enough to do the very big and complicated job of helping enough of the poor transition from poverty to financial independence to significantly move the needle on the poverty rate.

And with the renewed attacks on the poor by Romney surrogates like Gingrich, Santorum and Ryan during summer 2012, it is important to correct the hateful stereotypes from those who think it is great sport to ridicule and lie about those least able to defend themselves. The GOP has become expert at bullying, maligning and intimidation of poor, vulnerable Americans or those with whom they disagree, as illustrated by the following sad but true examples. While speaking at the Ozark Tea Party Rally, board member Inge Marler obviously felt the following joke was appropriate.

"A Black kid asks his Mom, 'Mama, what is a democracy?' Well, son, that be when White folks work every day so us po' folks can get all our benefits. But, Mama, don't the White folks get mad about that? They sho' do, Son. And that's called racism."

Dave Bartholomew, Virginia Beach Republican Party chairman, forwarded the following e-mail to his contact list.

My Dog

"I went down this morning to sign up my dog for welfare. At first the lady said, 'Dogs are not eligible to draw welfare'. So I explained to her that

Poverty, Politics and Race (The View From Down Here)

my dog is Black, unemployed, lazy, can't speak English, and has no frigging clue who his Daddy is. So she looked in her policy book to see what it takes to qualify...

My Dog gets his first check Friday. Is this a great country or what?"

Both of these winners were forced to resign their positions. And though shocking, there was nothing surprising about their attitudes toward the poor who are used to being the target of this kind of ignorance and racism. It was a surprise, however, that even the Republicans and Tea Party leaders found Marler and Bartholomew's behavior offensive enough to take action, given their usual tolerance for hate and racism for the past 4 years, since Obama's election.

"Working Poor" is the description given to most low-income Americans because they work. Many do so under the most difficult circumstances; often on part-time, minimum wage, sub minimum wages and tips, or commission only jobs with no benefits. These jobs usually require them to work evenings, weekends, and holidays when it is hardest and most costly to find childcare and transportation. In small, rural communities where no public transportation exists, private coordinated transportation companies charge so much per trip that it could easily require the greater part of a day's wage just to cover transportation to and from work.

Poverty, Politics and Race (The View From Down Here)

Newt Gingrich, though he certainly knows better, returned to his ugly attacks on poor families, children, and his refrain that President Obama was the "Food Stamp President"; claiming Obama put more people on food stamps than any President in history. However, the recent record holder is President George W. Bush. And, of course, Newt would never ever admit to any correlation between the devastating economic condition in which President George W. Bush left the country and the greatly increased need for food stamps before Obama was inaugurated.

At the time President Clinton left office, he had reduced the number of Food Stamp recipients by 8.2%. Then Bush took office in 2001, erased the 8.2% advantage that Clinton left and added 11% more for a total growth in food stamps under his administration of 19.2%. The percent of Americans on food stamps under President Obama was 18.1%. It is even more important to make the distinction that the high percentage of food stamp recipients, during the Bush terms, was attributable to his economic policies. And since America's economic mess of 2008 that created a new class of poor from millions of middle income Americans who lost their jobs due to those same policies, Bush shares the responsibility for the 18.1% credited to Obama.

Gingrich at that time chose to double down on his previous comments that poor children should be hired as janitors at their schools because they have no adults in their lives that get up and go to work unless involved in illegal activities. More recently, he stated, "Hire 30 some kids to work in

Poverty, Politics and Race (The View From Down Here)

the schools for the price of one janitor, and those 30 kids would be a lot less likely to drop out... They'd learn to show up for work". In addition to being insulting beyond belief, without sub, sub minimum wage for poor children, based on the calculation of pay for 30 children compared with the wage of one school janitor, it was a ridiculous thankfully unachievable idea. Further, what would happens to the adult janitor, likely a parent, who would lose his or her job under the Gingrich proposal? I guess it was not a valuable lesson after all to have an adult to show the children the value of work, since he had no qualms about taking the janitor's job in order to exploit children at slave wages.

And finally those opposed to Obama's American Recovery and Reinvestment Act (stimulus) program continue to claim it failed to create jobs, though Congress is well aware of the actual job numbers from the program.

Instead, it was one of Obama's best achievements; because the infusion of critical federal funding, at a time the economy was at its weakest, prevented wholesale layoffs at the state level and created hundreds of thousands of new jobs. The over $800,000 in CSBG stimulus funding, added to Capital Area Community Action Agency's $500,000 annual basic CSBG award, and for the first time provided a meaningful level of funding to help the poor achieve real family self-sufficiency goals.

The Agency created a model Weatherization job training and placement program in partnership

Poverty, Politics and Race (The View From Down Here)

with the region's Workforce Plus Agency and Tallahassee Community College. It resulted in Capital Area Community Action Agency being recognized as the top CAA job creator in the 2nd quarter of 2010. The Agency, for the first time had enough funds to extend more job training services to all 8 counties served, and removed transportation barriers that existed in 7 of the small, more rural or coastal counties. This allowed Certified Nursing Assistants (CNA) training, GED, computer, and micro-enterprise classes to be scheduled in these counties and extended job opportunities to pockets of North Florida that would not have been possible without these additional stimulus funds.

The ARRA (or stimulus) Weatherization equipped the Agency to finally hire enough Weatherization Program staff to properly monitor and direct the work of over 25 additional contractors in completing over a thousand energy efficiency projects for elderly, disabled, and working poor households in 6 counties. This was the truth about the work that was really being done in communities throughout America by dedicated community based organizations that get a lot of blame for anything that goes wrong for the poor, but very little credit for their decades of hard work under very challenging circumstances, to improve the lives of this nation's poor.

If Congress would have increased basic funding for programs like CSBG, weatherization, Head Start, mortgage and housing assistance grants, Community Development Block Grants to meaningful levels, instead of one-time stimulus, the

Poverty, Politics and Race (The View From Down Here)

nation could have been put on the road to real recovery much sooner.

Safety net programs create a variety of jobs in local communities, from social services that connect poor children and families to services to improve the quality of their lives, to Community Development Block Grants that fund housing and infrastructure jobs. The Community Development Block Grant Programs resurface roads, provide community and senior centers, rehabilitate housing in low income neighborhoods, and support the development of community health centers, along with the jobs created or retained. Housing and Urban Development (HUD) programs make affordable housing available to the poor, while creating jobs required to manage those properties and services.

I could do a book on the linkages between these safety net programs and jobs, but I think the point has been made. These programs improve people's lives, the quality of our neighborhoods, and strengthen the economic foundations of our communities, while breaking the chain of poverty. They, also, prepare new generations with the necessary skills to succeed in a free market economy.

Finally, the devastation of the northeastern United States by hurricane Sandy, an area not as used to the horrors of hurricanes as Florida, was a sharp and heartbreaking reminder of a very important role of the federal government. Without the disaster relief coordination and resources of

Poverty, Politics and Race (The View From Down Here)

FEMA, states hit by disasters that destroy their infrastructure and immobilize their human resources would be left completely helpless.

We are not a collection of autonomous states able to stand alone, but the United States of America. The three branches of the federal government Executive, Judicial, and Legislative. Ensure continuity of services, rights, and protection from enemies within and abroad for all Americans. The role of the federal government is to be an effective partner in this endeavor; and particularly at times when the interests of Americans can only be protected when we work together as a nation.

Poverty, Politics and Race (The View From Down Here)

Chapter 5

Perspective from the Past

Poverty, Politics and Race (The View From Down Here)

During the over six decades of my life, I have witnessed many of the more dramatic events in the civil rights movement and African American history – in the South. Jim Crow laws had a choke hold on almost every segment of our lives. And, there is a fear today that we may be returning to that era.

In the 1950s and 60s, the reality of my youth in Birmingham was segregated housing, neighborhoods, schools, movie theaters, public facilities, restaurants, restrooms, transportation and of course churches. As already noted, books used in the classrooms at the schools black children attended were outdated, "hand-me downs" from the "white" schools which were provided the new, updated text books. Yet, the teachers were determined that they would not allow these road blocks or our poverty to hinder their goal to graduate well-educated students. It was as though black and white families lived in parallel universes in the South, with little overlap. Back then, teachers were very highly regarded professionals by parents and the community. The segregated Black community was close knit, and teachers actually knew the parents of their students. A child did not dare "sass" the teacher or step out of line at school; or they would risk the wrath of God when word reached the parents.

Blacks generally were seen in white neighborhoods only when their jobs required them to be there. On occasion, carloads of white teens would sometimes find themselves driving along streets of Black neighborhoods; often for no reason except to taunt. I found myself the victim of such

Poverty, Politics and Race (The View From Down Here)

taunting early one evening as I walked the few blocks to my family's home. My mom's rule was – "Don't let night catch you away from home." On this day I visited longer than planned with friends, and broke her rule. The car drove past with the occupants yelling racial slurs and obscenities. When the car turned to come back, I ran onto the nearest porch, banging on the door and yelling, "Mama, open the door!" Thinking this was where I actually lived, the car sped off. I ran home; and, thereafter, followed Mama's rule, with no exception.

For most of my childhood, it seemed the Black people in Birmingham accepted that this was just the way things had to be if we did not want trouble; and, instead, a peaceful co-existence. Some people coped by hiding their anger in a bottle, some took out their frustration and anger in violence turned on each other or Black on Black violence; while others looked to God and the church for answers. With laws that institutionalized apartheid here in the American South, for many years Blacks felt they had no options besides accepting these conditions.

The acceptance of these circumstances reminds me of a quote by Reverend Al Sharpton that "A lot of things were acceptable until we decided not to accept them." I don't remember my exact age when the Black people in Birmingham decided they were no longer willing to accept hand-me-down text books, separate, but unequal conditions of our schools, "White Only" and "Negro" restrooms and water fountains, backdoor balcony entrances for movie theaters, lack of access to public

Poverty, Politics and Race (The View From Down Here)

parks and pools, and Jim Crow laws that barred our parents from exercising their rights to full citizenship. But I certainly remember there was a real sense of pride when it finally happened.

We were no longer in the background, staying quietly in our place. It was a shock to the system of the White power structure that had until then maintained this two-tier existence for White and Black residents, with seeming quiet acceptance and little to no resistance.

Then those Black ministers under the local leadership of Rev. Fred Shuttlesworth, and out-of-town "agitators" that included Rev. Martin Luther King Jr. and Rev. Ralph Abernathy lit a spark and started a movement. Suddenly we were looking forward to Thursday nights and attending Mass Meetings at the Sixteenth Street Baptist Church, with our mother, in downtown Birmingham. There, we would hear rousing rally speeches by these historic ministers and leaders. The meetings opened with everyone standing as the Birmingham Mass Choir led us in singing "Lift Every Voice and Sing," known as the Negro National Anthem; and closed with all of us standing arms linked, singing "We Shall Overcome."

These meetings moved our parents to activism, whether by joining non-violent marches, coordinating or driving in car pools transporting marchers and picketers to assigned locations, preparing meals in the 16th Street Baptist Church basement for demonstrators, staffing the movement

Poverty, Politics and Race (The View From Down Here)

office, or encouraging and supporting participation by their teenage children.

My two younger sisters and I became part of the children's movement, the marches, and the picket lines in front of department stores that refused to serve us at their lunch counters and denied us access to restrooms, even though the dollars spent at these stores by Black customers were just as green as those of White customers.

Fear and intimidation were the usual tactics employed to keep the downtrodden in their proper place. In the beginning these tactics were more subtle. Adults were threatened with job loss if they were found to be participants. Many of the adults, who were dependent on white employers for jobs in order to care for their families, conducted their activities in the background while their children took more visible, prominent roles in the movement.

When job threats did not reduce participation or our fervor, crosses were burned on the lawns of Black leaders by the Klan to warn that much worse would follow if their activities continued. When the desired behavior did not result, cross burnings were followed by the bombing of these activists' homes.

It was an ever present concern that you never knew who the Klan was. It was as likely that White law enforcement officers, elected white leaders, and even the white pastor who preached the gospel of Christ on Sunday, donned the white robe and hood to terrorize the Black community on

Poverty, Politics and Race (The View From Down Here)

Saturday night. And the Klan was likely made up of more Democrats than Republicans in the early years. As the Democratic Party became more activist on issues of voting and civil rights in the mid to late 1960s, southern White supremacists fled the Democratic Party and became Republicans.

Even so, the threats and attacks only served to stiffen the Black community's resolve, as in the spiritual that became a theme song of the movement, "Ain't Gonna Let Nobody Turn Me 'Round."

The tensions in Birmingham, Montgomery, Selma and other parts of the South burst into the national and international conscience, with images of vicious police dogs and fire hoses at full blast turned on peaceful demonstrators; and far worse, the bombing of the 16th Street Baptist Church which killed four little girls that Sunday morning in 1963. The bigotry and racial hatred exhibited by Whites could no longer be ignored.

The horror of those events finally moved President John F. Kennedy to push for Congressional action to ensure that the human and civil rights of Black Americans would be protected; even if local law enforcement could not be counted on to do so. Our hearts were broken in November 1963 when our beloved President was assassinated in Dallas, Texas. It, then, fell to President Lyndon Johnson to carry out the agenda started under President Kennedy. With courage and commitment, in spite of threats of political repercussions, President Lyndon Johnson_ a Texan

Poverty, Politics and Race (The View From Down Here)

pushed the passage of the Civil Rights Act of 1964 and the Voting Rights Act of 1965 through Congress.The Economic Opportunity Act, the centerpiece of President Johnson's War on Poverty, was passed and signed into law on August 20, 1964; and introduced the Community Action Anti-Poverty Programs and Head Start. A young civil rights attorney, Marian Wright (Edelman), was particularly effective in calling attention to the third world conditions of the poor in the Mississippi Delta and successfully introduced Head Start services in that state. Her testimony before a Senate Sub-committee and a poverty tour of the Delta created a powerful ally in then Senator Robert Kennedy; and focused the nation's attention on the poorest Americans...children. Passionate advocacy in their behalf became her life's work as founder of the national Children's Defense Fund.

Marian Wright Edelman with the author at Black Community Crusade for Children Conference in Birmingham

Poverty, Politics and Race (The View From Down Here)

Rev. Martin Luther King and the Southern Christian Leadership Conference (SCLC) kicked off a Poor People's Campaign in November 1967 and planned a Poor People's March on Washington to convince Congress to pass an Economic Bill of Rights for the poor. Before the march could take place, Rev. King was assassinated on April 4, 1968 at the Lorraine Hotel in Memphis, Tennessee.

I was a college senior living in Atlanta when I heard the shocking, painful news that another hero had been struck down; and several neighborhoods went up in flames from the raw anger that gripped the Black community and the nation over the senseless murder of the peace maker. Sadly, the neighborhoods in flames were our own and did nothing meaningful to address the underlying hatred that led to Dr. King's death. And those, who violated the law to express their anguish over the injustice, lost the high ground on which we must stand to demand justice.

After Reverend King's assassination, the same three pictures could be found on the wall of almost any Black home entered in the South. They were Christ Jesus, President John F. Kennedy, and Reverend Martin Luther King, Jr.

In May 1968, the Poor People's March on Washington went on as planned, led by Rev. King's widow Coretta Scott King, Rev. Jesse Jackson, Rev. Abernathy and thousands of Americans of all races to honor the memory and mission of Rev. King, our fallen leader.

Poverty, Politics and Race (The View From Down Here)

In the 60's there was clear recognition that civil rights, voting rights and the right to economic justice and opportunities were the keys to ensuring a chance for all Americans to enjoy this country's promise. Today everything we fought for back then, to ensure a better future for generations to come, is again under attack by White Americans led by conservatives waving the banner of the Republican Party.

Since President Obama's election, it seems the singular goal of the Republican Party, GOP elected leaders, and the Tea Party is to erase every gain achieved since the '60s for minorities, women, and the poor. It seemed in 2012, they have specifically targeted Black-Americans, Hispanic-Americans and the poor for their renewed assault on rights guaranteed to all Americans under the Constitution.

The rallying cry of those in the South who wanted to maintain the segregated status quo of the past was "States Rights". That theme is gaining strength again in the Republican Party. Such a system gives states total autonomy over its residents and would in effect remove Constitutional guarantees of protection for the individual and provide unchecked power for each state. You don't need to look far to find examples of the terrible injustices this would cause if elected leaders in each state had the right to dictate whether Roe v. Wade, the Voting Rights Act, the Equal Opportunity Act, fair housing laws, the Affordable Care Act, and laws ensuring workplace safety and environmental justice were enforced.

Poverty, Politics and Race (The View From Down Here)

If not for the federal courts and federal government's ability to intervene when constitutionally guaranteed rights are threatened, the poor and other protected classes covered under the country's anti-discrimination laws would be rendered powerless to defend themselves. States rights during the Jim Crow era were just another way of saying, free states to discriminate against whoever they choose, whenever they choose.

Today we are in a battle for the heart and soul of our country to prevent the rollback of freedoms we all hold dear. The good old days for some are instead the bad old days of one of the darkest periods of our past for many, the era of Jim Crow.

And we have no wish to repeat that past.

Poverty, Politics and Race (The View From Down Here)

Chapter 6

Racial Hatred and the Church

Poverty, Politics and Race (The View From Down Here)

Sundays have been described as the most segregated day of the week long after integration became legal in areas of the country where it was previously banned. 2012 still finds most Americans worshipping in churches segregated by race. In a country, however, which takes great pride in religious freedom, I do not consider it a problem that we exercise our right to worship where and how we please.

The problem is the fact that the church, widely considered a place of refuge and comfort for the poor, embattled, sick, and grief stricken regardless of race or economic status, has been invaded by the same ugly, divisive rhetoric and behavior so prevalent in our politics and daily discourse today. Once upon a time, the church and religious leaders were among the first to take a stand against injustice. They came from cities throughout America and represented all races, religions, and ages to speak out against bigotry and maltreatment of the poor and vulnerable as the Bible directs.

Black pastors and churches were the backbone of the Civil Rights movement of the 1950s and 1960s. The Klan made sure these pastors and their families paid a heavy price for their activism and involvement with repeated bombings of their churches and homes.

It is a testament to their courage that they were not dissuaded from their mission to protect the vulnerable. The Southern Christian Leadership Conference (SCLC) was formed when Dr. Martin

Poverty, Politics and Race (The View From Down Here)

Luther King invited 60 Black ministers and leaders to Atlanta to create an ongoing organizational structure to lead, coordinate, and support the non-violent civil rights movement in the South. The most notable among these founders of the SCLC were Rev. Fred Shuttlesworth (Birmingham, Alabama), Rev. Joseph Lowery (Mobile, Alabama), Rev. Ralph Abernathy (Atlanta Georgia and Montgomery, Alabama), Rev. C.K. Steele (Tallahassee, Florida), Bayard Rustin – organizer of the New York branch of the Congress of Racial Equality and advisor to Rev. King, Ella Baker – national field secretary for the NAACP and advisor to Rev. King, and of course Rev. Martin Luther King. Rustin was also the chief organizer of the 1963 March on Washington in support of civil rights legislation in Congress.

During this era, the 16th Street Baptist Church stood apart as a beacon in downtown Birmingham for its role as the staging site for the movement. The planning, scheduling, and mobilization of car pools and volunteers for the marches, pickets, sit ins, and voter registration drives were coordinated at the 16th Street Baptist Church. It was there, as well, that the Thursday night Mass Meetings was held to rally the mostly Black residents of Birmingham with speeches and songs that stirred the souls of those in attendance to stay the course.

The Klan made repeated threats of violence against the church if these activities continued. Then, on Sunday – September 15, 1962, the 16th Street Baptist Church was bombed during Sunday

Poverty, Politics and Race (The View From Down Here)

morning service without regard for the families worshipping inside. That bomb blast took the lives of 4 young Black girls – Addie Mae Collins (14), Cynthia Wesley (14), Carole Robertson (14), and Denise McNair (11). Four members of the United Klans of America_ Bobby Frank Cherry, Thomas Blanton, Herman Frank Cash, and Robert Chambliss – became suspects in this early act of terrorism in our country.

Though it took over 4 decades, Chambliss, Blanton and Cherry were finally brought to justice and convicted for their roles in these murders, thanks to the untiring efforts of the FBI and local prosecutors between 1977 and 2001. Cash, who passed an FBI polygraph test and was never charged, died in 1994.

The hate speech and references to the use of Second Amendment remedies by the GOP and Tea Party leaders since the election of Barack Obama in 2008 and his 2009 inauguration, is a reminder of how quickly the hate speech of the past turned into actual violence. I am also reminded of the number of times older black women expressed their fears for Obama's safety, during the 2008 Presidential campaign. The memory of the racial hatred that cut short the lives of too many of their past heroes made them anxious for this handsome, well-spoken, intelligent young man that they cared about like their own child, though they had never met him.

Since his election, the verbal attacks have become more vicious, even from those you would

Poverty, Politics and Race (The View From Down Here)

least expect such hate speech – White religious leaders.

Arizona pastor Stephen Anderson declared from his pulpit in 2012, "I hate Barack Obama!" To make sure his congregation had no misunderstanding of his animosity toward America's first Black President, he doubled down by explaining that his statement did not mean he just hates what Obama stands for. "No", he stated, "I hate the person. I hate him!" This kind of openly expressed venom from a supposed man of God toward the President of the United States, with no fear of retribution, is unprecedented.

Then there are the regular assaults and insults against the sitting President by anonymous bloggers such as "Kill Da Nigger", "Nigger President", "Bring back lynching", and one posting that stated, "I'm hoping someone will do his public duty by putting a bullet through Obama's head". Statements like these are beyond the pale and make the fears expressed by many Black grandmothers in 2008 seem not so far-fetched.

And most recently, Florida pastor Terry Jones erected a gallows at his church and hung an image of President Obama in effigy. It is incomprehensible to me that a church pastor and a church would not have had second thoughts about such an action if its mission had any resemblance to the charge given in the Bible to people of faith.

I have been equally astounded by the lack of expressed outrage from the religious community

Poverty, Politics and Race (The View From Down Here)

over these hateful acts and the brazen behavior of those who call themselves religious leaders. The church represents the last vestige of civility in a humane society. Therefore, the collective silence, instead of loud condemnation of such behavior by religious leaders, sends a scary message about where we are headed as a nation. It did not help matters when leaders of the Republican Party announced publicly that the one thing that united them in the 2012 Presidential election was their hatred for President Obama.

But, it is particularly troubling when religious leaders lower their standards to the least common denominator instead of setting the example in word and deed for tolerance and goodwill. Evangelicals and Republican values voters claim to be steeped in their religious faith. Yet, many of these same leaders did little to foster civility, and instead joined in the vitriolic attacks against the President.

It is likewise shocking, that many of these faith-based leaders strongly opposed extending a safety net to the poor, health services for the sick, and food stamps for the hungry, though the basic tenets of the Christian faith demand that believers extend help to those in need.

The most genuine demonstration of commitment to faith and mission was demonstrated by the Nuns on a Bus campaign led by Sister Simone Campbell, President of the National Social Justice Lobby. The nuns were unable to sit silently after the release of Congressman Paul Ryan's draft

Poverty, Politics and Race (The View From Down Here)

of the House budget that would give even larger tax cuts to the rich, with these excesses paid for with cuts and elimination of essential programs for poor and middle-income Americans. It signaled a call to action, and the Nuns on a Bus tour was launched. The purpose was to remind good Catholics like Ryan that the Catholic Church has as an important mission to help, not hurt, the poor. Ryan's draconian cuts to programs for the poor in the House Budget and his belief that providing basic crisis assistance is like giving the poor a "hammock" made it clear the church's message of empathy and a helping hand for the poor was not getting through.

Bachman and most House Republicans even voted against extending unemployment benefits to millions of Americans who lost their jobs due to the fiscal crisis caused by their policies. Both Ryan and Bachman profess to being committed to their religious faiths and the principles and values that form the foundation. Their actions, however, do not reflect the basic tenets of their faith. Both show disdain for the poor, most of whom are the "working poor" who earn so little on back breaking jobs that they still qualify for food stamps and Medicaid for health services not provided by their employer. Nor do they distinguish between the willing worker who cannot find a job in a still stagnant economy, and those who refuse to work.

What would the Republican Party propose to address child hunger among poor children to replace massive cuts to SNAP and the school breakfast and lunch program in their budget? And,

Poverty, Politics and Race (The View From Down Here)

what about the low-income elderly who after many years of hard work, and finally in retirement, are struggling to live on poverty level social security or pension checks? Would Bachman apply her work-or-starve principle to the elderly and disabled, as well?

A major problem with Ryan and Bachman, as with many Republicans who vigorously support their positions, is that they actually believe the stereotypes they have created about the poor. That's the charitable explanation. Or they are heartless and just do not care about those who are not like them. As a minister's wife and a Christian, I would have preferred to be charitable and believe the former, but their actions implied something far less commendable.

And, finally, where are the unified voices from the coalition of churches and the SCLC who were so effective in the past in bringing the needs of the poor and disenfranchised to the forefront and brokering solutions? In the 50s and 60s, Black, White, Hispanic, Protestant, Catholic, Jewish and Muslim leaders stood together against the extreme violence in the South and demanded change. What is required for that same solidarity against hate and violence today, irrespective of political ideology?

If anyone should have been expected to stand and speak out for justice and respect for the basic dignity of all Americans, in the face of all out attacks on the poor, civil, human, and voting rights, it should have been our faith leaders. Though churches may be quietly active in each of their local communities, in the mold of "thinking globally and

Poverty, Politics and Race (The View From Down Here)

acting locally", the openly expressed hate speech and demands for violence have become so prevalent that it requires religious leaders to respond in a more unified and loud voice.

This is still a country in which most Americans believe we can solve almost any problem when we approach it with civility and basic respect for the dignity of even those with whom we disagree.

Poverty, Politics and Race (The View From Down Here)

Chapter 7

The Real Class Warfare

Poverty, Politics and Race (The View From Down Here)

Grover Norquist, Congressional Republicans, and Mitt Romney tried to lay the full burden for the state of the economy on the poor and middle income Americans, and no responsibility for the wealthy banks, Wall Street, and corporations that caused the mess. They continued to push for huge tax breaks for the wealthy and adhered religiously to their no tax pledge to Norquist. They insisted that the wealthiest 2% of Americans were the "job creators" and any tax increase would lead to massive layoffs, deepen the recession, and erase any progress toward an economic recovery.

Any attempts by Democrats at raising revenues by asking the wealthiest Americans to pay a little more in taxes to prevent greater hardship on middle and low-income Americans were met with GOP charges of "class warfare" or redistribution of wealth. At the same time, these same Republicans saw no irony in their own budget recommendations that added to the wealth of the already rich by lowering their tax burdens further, while cutting programs and opposing tax relief for middle income and poor Americans.

For more than a decade corporate CEOs have been filling their pockets with multi-million dollar bonuses, even as they were tanking the American economy thanks to the trickle down economic policies of George W. Bush, and a Republican Congress, supported by most of the Blue Dog Democrats in Washington. It should have been no surprise, then, that eighty percent (80%) of America's wealth was controlled in 2012 by 10% of Americans; while 90% of Americans shared only

Poverty, Politics and Race (The View From Down Here)

20% of this country's wealth. That fact clearly disproved the Republican's argument that when the wealthy is swimming in money, jobs are plentiful and everyone shares in their prosperity.

Instead during this period of great prosperity by the wealthy, they sat on their wealth, created no jobs, almost toppled the American economy with their greed, and created the widest income gap between the rich and all other Americans in recent history. By 2012, America's poverty rate had risen to its highest level in over two decades, at 15.1%.

Just fourteen years earlier, President Clinton was ending his second term, after having presided over a period of real prosperity for all Americans. When Clinton handed over the keys to the White House to President George W. Bush in January 2001, he was credited with having left a budget surplus of $230 billion that Bush quickly squandered on two wars and tax cuts. Under Clinton, the top tax rate for the rich was 39%. The unemployment rate was 4.2% when he left office. Eight years later when President Bush left office, he had cut the top tax rate for the rich to 35% and left an 8.2% unemployment rate.

With a 39% tax rate for the "job creators", the Clinton administration created 22.5 million jobs_ a thirty year record. Clearly, President Clinton's economic accomplishments with a higher tax rate completely destroyed the GOP position that increasing the highest tax rate by 4% to the level under Clinton would be an economic disaster. And over 60% of Americans agreed that it would be

Poverty, Politics and Race (The View From Down Here)

preferable to increase taxes for the rich to pay their fair share in reducing the deficit, than raising taxes and cutting services to poor and middle income Americans.

In spite of all of the evidence to the contrary, Congressional Republicans stuck to their talking points that the only way to heal the economy was to give more money to the rich while cutting resources to the poorest Americans. In doing so, President Clinton was proven correct when he stated at the Democratic Convention that this is all about arithmetic. And the Republican numbers just don't add up.

Worse, Paul Ryan and the Republicans weren't just opposing the rate increase to 39% from the Bush rate of 35%. They actually wanted to reward their wealthy friends with a tax rate of 25%, an additional 10% tax cut. Romney, among the top earners, agreed with the Ryan and House recommendation to lower the top tax rate to 25% - creating even greater income inequality. At the same time these so-called job creators, who like Romney, rarely paid anywhere close to the 35% rate with all the tax loop holes available to the wealthy, continue to negatively impact the U.S. unemployment rate by shipping American jobs overseas.

Absolute war has been declared against labor unions by the political right and wealthy corporations. Why? There should be no mystery. Unions were created to protect the rights of the worker – including the right to a fair wage, health

Poverty, Politics and Race (The View From Down Here)

and other benefits, and regulations to ensure workplace safety. Greedy corporations, with a singular profit motive above all else, naturally would have the opposite goal. Therefore, while demonizing unions which created America's middle class, these corporations were closing manufacturing plants in America for decades and shipping jobs to countries where they could legally benefit from "slave labor", with no labor laws or work place safety regulations. In poor countries, American manufacturers are able to exploit people living in such impoverished conditions that even pay as low as a dollar or less an hour is acceptable. These companies produce merchandise that is then imported to America and sold in stores like Wal-Mart, while unemployed Americans saw jobs being exported to produce these goods.

The Republicans, corporate giants, and the U.S. Chamber of Commerce have tried to lay the blame at the feet of President Obama for their decades long excesses and lobbying for financial policies highly beneficial to corporate America and devastating to the rest of us. These same corporate leaders poured hundreds of millions of dollars into the Romney campaign, and Romney Super PACs, in a determined effort to defeat Obama, who proposed the expiration of the Bush tax cuts for earnings above $250,000.

Further, President Obama's jobs record has been the opposite of the picture painted by Republicans. When President Obama was inaugurated, America was bleeding 800,000 jobs per month. He introduced the American Recovery and

Poverty, Politics and Race (The View From Down Here)

Reinvestment Act (ARRA), passed by a democratically controlled Congress. It cut taxes for small businesses and 95% of Americans; provided emergency funding to states to prevent up to 300,000 teacher layoffs; sent funds to local governments to protect thousands of law enforcement, firefighter, and public sector jobs; and funded weatherization and clean energy jobs. Altogether, the President's ARRA initiatives created 3.3 million jobs in America.

It is important to point out that the emergency bailout funds to states, many controlled by Republican Governors and Legislatures were necessary because of the desperate condition of these states' budgets, in order to prevent massive public sector employee layoffs. The drain on revenues for most of these states can be traced back to a state level tax cutting trend established two decades ago, with no plan for replacing lost state revenues.

As with today's Republicans, the states had to cut revenues for services because the tax cuts were unsustainable and penalized residents with high job losses, and draconian cuts to programs for the poor. In Florida, trust funds like the Sadowsky Affordable Housing Trust Fund, created with documentary stamp fees paid on home mortgages – was drained to plug the state budget deficit caused by years of bad budget policies by state leaders. As a result, millions of Florida residents were robbed of dedicated funds for safe, livable housing conditions for poor, elderly, and disabled Floridians. Many of the job losses blamed on President Obama,

Poverty, Politics and Race (The View From Down Here)

therefore, were actually caused by poor budget policies at the state level. Many of these states were controlled by Republican governors and legislatures whose policies created the states' terrible economic conditions.

President Obama's economic policies, contrary to the Republican talking points, added 4.5 million private sector jobs between 2010 and 2012, 504,000 manufacturing jobs over the same period, and saved over a million auto industry jobs with his Auto Rescue Program that provided federal assistance to protect American jobs at General Motors and Chrysler. Whole state economies depended on these auto companies and related businesses.

Yet Romney, in a New York Times op-ed, declared "Let Detroit Go Bankrupt." Of course after the President's plan proved to be such a stunning success, Romney tried to rewind, wipe out everyone's memory and pretend he not only favored the President's auto industry bailout, but was actually the initiator of the plan. With Michigan and Ohio so dependent on auto industry jobs and such important states in determining the outcome of the 2012 Presidential election, it was no surprise that Romney tried to make voters in those states forget he opposed any help for the auto industry. This "Etch-a-Sketch" moment was very convenient for Romney to attempt to erase his lack of support from the public's memory, as he struggled to convince middle and low-income Americans he was sensitive to their needs.

Poverty, Politics and Race (The View From Down Here)

However, the fact that Romney supported the Paul Ryan and GOP budget plan that widened the income inequality between top income earners and other Americans did nothing to dispel that perception. At the same time that the wealthy received this huge largesse of corporate welfare, those who really needed the government safety net were being shafted in the Ryan-Romney-Republican proposed budget. That budget proposed the following.

1. Cuts in Pell grants to 2008 levels, denying many students dependent on that financial assistance a pathway to higher education.
2. Block granting Medicaid to states which have trouble managing their own budgets, and indexing the program for inflation and population growth, with no recognition of the actual growth in healthcare cost. This was a back door cut to funds available to ensure health services for the poor.
3. Deep cuts to the Food Stamp and other safety net programs which would leave countless children, elderly and disabled poor hungry in America.
4. The privatization of Medicare by turning it into a voucher program that could cost the elderly over $6000 annually in cost not covered by the voucher, and leaves them hostage to rising private insurance and healthcare costs. This would be particularly problematic since the Ryan Plan also proposed the repeal of President

Poverty, Politics and Race (The View From Down Here)

Obama's Affordable Care Act, scheduled to take full effect in 2014 with maximum benefits.

Therefore, I found it difficult to understand how the Republicans had been so successful in the past with their arguments in favor of these cuts; particularly with older Americans who stood to lose so much with that plan.

All evidence showed that tax cuts and deregulation had led to unprecedented profits and wealth for corporations. At the same time, Americans lost jobs in record numbers. I wondered how these folks looked at themselves in the mirror?! There was no way to explain corporate America's behavior except pure, unadulterated greed. Further, it was the height of hypocrisy by Republicans to create the conditions that led to such a disparity between the incomes of the top 2% compared to 98% of us, while blaming Democrats for class warfare.

It is even harder to understand that almost half of Americans have been willing to either ignore the facts, or are so uninformed that the Republicans were able to convince them to act against their own interests in support of recommendations that only benefit the wealthy. The GOP Citizens United Super PACs and the almost billion dollars they pumped into Republican campaigns is a clear indication why these elected officials are so committed to the interests of these wealthy donors. But it is a total mystery how average Americans could be convinced these laws that benefit the selfish interests of the wealthy are also in their best interests.

Poverty, Politics and Race (The View From Down Here)

It was not the Democrats who redistributed the wealth. It was instead the economic policies of the GOP that created the conditions in which those who were already rich got richer, while almost everyone else was one or two paychecks away from mortgage foreclosure, homelessness, bankruptcy, and the loss of everything they had built over a lifetime of hard work. And, to add insult to injury, the wealthy seemed to feel no shame as they sought to deny help to the poorest among us in order to enlarge their share of the pie.

If there is a silent majority that feels America is better than the "haves and have even less" country envisioned by Republican leaders, it is past time to make their voices heard. We deserve an America in which the tent is big enough to include all in the opportunities for a better life. That was not the America the Republican Party was offering in 2012.

Chapter 8

Leveling the Credit Playing Field

Poverty, Politics and Race (The View From Down Here)

Middle-income Americans, many of whom depend on credit for large purchases, have over the past decade become as much the victims of legalized loan sharking as the poor. Middle-income Blacks and other minorities, in particular, have been subjected to unfair and predatory lending practices since the introduction of "redlining" in 1937.

Redlining is the practice by banks of color coding neighborhoods with high minority populations, regardless of income, and applying much higher interest rates, less favorable terms, and more stringent criteria in order to qualify for loans. Few wealthy Americans can relate to this problem because they either have all the cash they need or easy access to it. They have easy access to capital to purchase multi-million dollar homes in every region of the country; some with car elevators. If a family member needs a job they buy a company. If the kids need cash, they set up million dollar trust funds. Cars no problem and there is so much money left that there are not enough U.S. banks to hold it all; and some has to be sent to live in the Cayman's or Swiss Bank accounts.

However, debt is a very real problem for most middle, moderate, and low-income Americans, who wish billionaires like the Koch brothers and Sheldon Adelson cared enough about the plight of average Americans to invest a small fraction of the money spent during the election in rebuilding impoverished communities. Good or bad, most average Americans rely on credit for large purchases or high cost emergency expenses like medical costs, home and car purchases, major home

Poverty, Politics and Race (The View From Down Here)

or car repairs, unexpected increases in college tuition, or small business shortfalls or expenses.

Since 2000, subprime mortgage loans were real wealth builder for the banking industry and Wall Street; but devastating for homeowners trapped in these high risk mortgages. Wells Fargo Bank, Bank of America and its subsidiary, Countrywide, were the biggest offenders.

Studies of mortgage loan practices of Well Fargo revealed that upper-income Black borrowers were almost twice as likely to end up with subprime mortgages as low-income White borrowers. Loan officers referred to Blacks as "mud people" and subprime loans as "ghetto loans". Seven decades of redlining practiced against Blacks and other minorities created an environment that allowed Wells Fargo to primarily market subprime mortgages to the minority community. Many of those borrowers were also deceived through Countrywide's marketing campaign to refinance existing mortgages with much more favorable and savings, but instead ended up in more risky adjustable rate loans disguised as more favorable loan proposals. They were convinced that the savings in interest to pay off other higher interest rate loans or credit cards made refinancing their mortgage a win-win. These borrowers, instead, became victims of subprime mortgage skims that beginning in 2008 resulted in record numbers of bankruptcies and foreclosures, as rapidly escalating interest rates made mortgages completely unaffordable.

Poverty, Politics and Race (The View From Down Here)

Countrywide's marketing pitch, in televised commercials, promised to relieve those with major mortgage or credit card debt of high interest rates and to provide lower monthly payments through debt refinancing with them. Their main interest, however, was to snare the unwitting borrower in the subprime net of Countrywide and Bank of America for higher company profits and commissions for loan officers. At the same time, borrowers were being trapped unknowingly into refinancing fixed rate loans for adjustable or variable rate products. Loan officers received large commissions or bonuses that were major incentives to close as many of these deals as possible, regardless of the harm these deceptive practices caused the borrower.

The boom in subprime mortgages over the past two decades led to high stock prices for those trading on the misfortune of others, with Countrywide CEOs among the highest paid in the nation. Even when their practices began to be questioned, Bank of America and Countrywide did nothing to change course, according to a quote from the article "Inside the Countrywide Lending Spree" by Gretchen Morgenson.

In a 2010 discrimination lawsuit filed by Illinois Attorney General Lisa Madigan against Countrywide, she charged that even Blacks and Latinos qualified for other types of loans were given subprime products at higher interest rates and fees. She stated, "It's disturbingly clear that if you were an African-American or Latino borrower who

Poverty, Politics and Race (The View From Down Here)

walked into a Countrywide, you likely paid more for your mortgage than a white borrower".

The behavior of Countrywide and Bank of America proved so egregious that Madigan and the U.S. Department of Justice were able to get a settlement of $335 million. A more preferable outcome would have been criminal charges and prison time for those responsible for orchestrating this plan that so completely destroyed so many families' lives, and even larger monetary damages. But even a tap on the hand is better than no penalty at all.

A whole industry, referred to as the "poverty industry", was created during this same period to build wealth through the victimization of the poor. The most common of these businesses that suddenly took bloom in inner-city neighborhoods were Payday loan, Title loan, and refund anticipation loan companies – some of which were little more than loan shark operations with legal standing. All exploited the poor who had no other options to address emergency financial needs. Unlike middle, and upper-income families who have other family members or professional connections, or their own income and credit record to give them access to needed cash, the poor usually have no such backup system of support due to generational poverty. They are, therefore, easy targets for the predatory loan industry.

These companies claim to provide a valuable service to these low-income borrowers. And since the financial circumstances and lack of credit

Poverty, Politics and Race (The View From Down Here)

worthiness for most of their clients would likely disqualify them for loans at the traditional financial institutions, they are providing a service for a high risk borrower. However, these loans are designed with such extraordinarily high interest rates, penalties, and collateral that there is little chance anyone will be the loser, except the low-income borrowers.

Chances are good that the title loan company will end up owning the borrower's car, if the small short-term loan is not repaid in full within a relatively narrow time frame, with an exorbitant amount of interest added to the principle loan balance. The terms make it almost impossible for most people using these services to meet their loan obligation. Therefore, those who have the least must pay the highest prices for help when there is a financial emergency and no place else to turn except these predatory loan companies that build their fortunes on the misfortunes of others.

During the 1990's, title loan and Pay Day loan store fronts began to spring up in low-income neighborhoods or in business districts in close proximity to these neighborhoods with high concentrations of poor and minority residents. It is rare to see such businesses in middle and upper income neighborhoods and suburbs. Title and Pay Day loans are the most common of these high risk loan products which, with few exceptions, usually leave the borrowers in a deeper financial hole than they were before the loan.

Poverty, Politics and Race (The View From Down Here)

Title loans require the applicant to relinquish the title to their vehicle as collateral for the short term loan, and often require repayment within 30 days. The interest rate and fees can range from 36 to 250%, in some cases, requiring the low-income borrower to magically acquire 50% to double the amount actually borrowed in a very short period of time or risk the loss of the only tangible asset for the family. As a result, many title loans end with repossession of the loan recipient's car. Not a good outcome.

Payday loans require the applicant to provide a post dated check at the time of the loan advance that is sent to the bank for payment on the borrower's pay date. The repayment date can be as early as two weeks later. Repayment on the 2 week loan will include interest and fees of 36 to as much as 100%. The loan can be rolled over if unable to repay by the due date; but the interest and fees are compounded creating an ever growing debt that can sink the borrower into such a deep financial hole that it is impossible to climb out. No one with any other options would ever consider a title or payday loan that leaves the borrower's circumstances far worse after the loan.

Then there are the Refund Anticipation Loans. With e-filing and many opportunities for free tax preparation, it may be surprising and hard to believe that there are still so many low-income residents who are willing to forfeit 10% or more of their tax refund in order to receive it only a week or two early in the form of a loan. It's an indication of

Poverty, Politics and Race (The View From Down Here)

the daily desperation of people living on the financial edge.

The Internal Revenue Service, in partnership with organizations like the United Way, Community Action Agencies, Urban Leagues, and other community based organizations, has worked to create the Volunteer Income Tax Assistance (VITA) program for free tax prep and e-filing to give the poor an alternative to refund anticipation loans. These coalitions, in addition to free tax preparation also provide public education and awareness campaigns on the pitfalls of predatory lending and the availability of community VITA sites. The program ensures that low income families receive their Earned Income Tax Credits for increased and refunds without falling into the vicious predatory lending cycle.

Credit bureaus are another story, altogether. The three bureaus – Equifax, Trans Union, and Experian – have a lot of power over the lives of middle income Americans who depend on just the right credit score for access to low rate mortgages, mortgage refinancing, auto loans, and cash for important family needs. Credit bureaus, as currently structured, present a few problems of their own in allowing consumers full use of their credit.

First, they have too much power over the average consumer's life, and they are not infallible. They make mistakes. And because every lender in America uses the credit scores assigned to them by these three companies, they must thoroughly verify

Poverty, Politics and Race (The View From Down Here)

information added to consumers' credit histories and profiles. Further, when mistakes are reported, they must move with urgency to correct the error. That is not always the case, and creates major hardships for some families.

Second, credit bureaus have made it very difficult to report mistakes. Some years ago, there were credit bureau branch offices in most urban areas or regional offices within a reasonable travel distance to be easily accessible should a problem arise. Consumers could easily make contact and interact with human beings in resolving credit reporting issues. That is no longer true. In the internet age, complaints or error reports are made on-line or by mail, with little opportunity to track progress on the resolution of the problem or even to be assured that the information was received.

After filing, a response moves at such a snail's pace that it can seem as though the complaint fell into a black hole. And sometimes, it actually does.

About 8 years ago when refinancing my mortgage with my credit union for a more favorable rate, I was surprised to learn Equifax was reporting a lien for delinquent taxes on my property. My residence was my only real property and both insurance and assessed property taxes were included in the escrow as part of my monthly mortgage payment. Though the credit union was my mortgage holder and documented that the payments and escrow were up to date, my refinancing application could not proceed until I

Poverty, Politics and Race (The View From Down Here)

was able to correct the inaccurate report of a property tax lien on my credit report with Equifax.

A trip to the county property appraiser and tax collector's office revealed nothing to support the data on the credit report that was negatively affecting my credit score. The County Property Appraiser provided an official statement on letterhead verifying there was no lien on my home – the only property for which I had ownership interest. This allowed the mortgage refinancing to go forward, but there was still the problem of correcting the error on the Equifax report to prevent my credit score being lowered further.

I requested and received a copy of my credit report. Upon receipt it revealed that Equifax was reporting a property lien for delinquent tax payments on a piece of real estate in a small South Georgia town in which I never resided and never owned property. However, it was not enough to point out the fact I had maintained continuous residency in Florida for over 30 years, with the homestead exemptions to prove it. I had to also prove I was not the owner of the property in the little South Georgia town.

I was beyond frustrated. In an attempt to get to the bottom of this situation I took a leave day from my job to travel to Georgia with credit report in hand. At the office of the County Court Clerk, an exhaustive search was conducted of county property records with no property or deed listed in my name. It is very difficult to prove something that does not exist. Finally the very patient and kind county clerk

Poverty, Politics and Race (The View From Down Here)

located the property by the address and verified that the property in question was owned by a local family whose name bore no resemblance to mine.

Fortunately, I left with a statement from the County Clerk documenting their finding. Both the Court Clerk and I were puzzled at how Equifax could include completely incorrect information on my credit report, with no source information. I immediately submitted the proof of their error to the credit bureau by overnight mail, with a request that urgent attention be given to correcting my report and score. I received no acknowledgement that any action was ever taken despite repeated follow ups by phone, on-line, and by mail.

Two years later, when I requested a copy of my scores and a credit report from each of the three reporting agencies, the error still appeared on my Equifax report. It is likely that though much time and effort was devoted to following every requirement in the complaint process, the error likely remains to this date on my credit report. It was my opinion then, and remains my position today, that an organization with the power to damage consumers' financial reputation should be held to a higher standard of accuracy. Further, there should be some way to hold them accountable for such damage if prompt and deliberate action is not taken to correct errors once reported. I was fortunate that no such mistake was made by the other two reporting agencies. There is just too much power vested in these three credit reporting agencies when the scores they assign have the

Poverty, Politics and Race (The View From Down Here)

impact of controlling every important financial decision we make.

Likewise, for much too long, there has been very little oversight for the credit card industry. It has allowed this industry to become more and more abusive in the unilateral manner in which it changes terms, dramatically increases interest rates without warning, makes unannounced changes in credit limits, fees, penalties, payment schedules and locations, and adds services and fees without cardholder's permission or notice. The word service in customer service was often getting lost in the process, and consumers had few avenues for resolving disputes with their credit card company.

The near collapse of the U.S. economy due to abuses and behavior by the "too big to fail" financial industry left Washington no choice except to reform the way it regulated and monitored the country's major financial institutions. The system as designed in 2008 when the economy almost collapsed under the weight of questionable financial decisions and possibly criminal behavior, crystallized the need for comprehensive financial reform and regulations. Wall Street and the nation's largest banks made reckless decisions in order to accumulate more wealth and placed the financial well being of the country and all Americans at risk.

Therefore, in spite of vehement opposition from the GOP, Wall Street, and the financial industry, Obama's new Consumer Financial Protection Agency was approved by Congress in July 2010, as part of the Wall Street Regulatory

Poverty, Politics and Race (The View From Down Here)

Reform packet after many years of passionate, strong advocacy for such an agency by newly elected U.S. Senator from Massachusetts, Elizabeth Warren, in the November 2012 election.

President Obama named Richard Cordray director of the new Agency in a recess appointment in July 2011 to bypass Senate Republicans' plan to obstruct and block the appointment and delay start up of the Agency. The responsibilities of the Agency include oversight to prevent major violations of mortgage disclosure laws and infractions that could cause consumers to unwittingly sign up for the kind of risky subprime loans that led to the recent mortgage foreclosure fiasco. It will also monitor and handle consumer complaints on the credit card industry, credit bureaus, payday/ predatory lending practices, and other complaints on deceptive practices and products, and abusive behavior by other financial institutions and debt collectors. It will be part of a comprehensive consumer financial protection agency that will include financial oversight of Wall Street and the "too big to fail" banking industry by the Department of Treasury and the Federal Reserve.

We should not forget it was the massive deregulation of Wall Street and major financial institutions during George W. Bush's administration that led to the near crash of America's economy at the end of 2008. And for those of us languishing on the lower rungs of the income ladder, the American consumers finally have advocates to protect our financial well being by providing access to economic fairness.

Poverty, Politics and Race (The View From Down Here)

Congress must now find a way around Republican obstruction and fully confirm Mr. Cordray as the Agency Director, as an expression of unimpeded support for the important work he must do to protect the rights of American consumers.

Poverty, Politics and Race (The View From Down Here)

Chapter 9

Environmental Justice

Poverty, Politics and Race (The View From Down Here)

It just takes a drive through any urbanized area, in which there are distinct pockets of poverty, to note the location of the city's industrial parks and where the most incompatible development exists adjacent to surrounding neighborhoods. The immediate common pattern is that these developments – factories, power plants, medical waste incinerators, landfills, sewer plants, and like facilities that emit harmful chemical pollutants into the air, soil, or groundwater – are almost always located near low-income or modest income neighborhoods. It is rare to nonexistent that such facilities would be located or sited near upper income communities like the ones where corporate CEOs of such operations would reside.

Even in cases in which these facilities were built prior to the development of the neighborhood, it would be rare to find upscale developments built in close proximity to land zoned for heavy manufacturing or industrial uses. There are three reasons. First, the developer would not choose an area to build high value homes that would prevent the ability to sell the homes at top dollar value. Second, the type buyer that can afford to purchase homes at that market rate would have no interest in making that kind of investment in an area where the property would not maintain its high property values.

And third, buyers for properties at that price point would have done their research on the community and would come to the table with a preference for the kind of neighborhood, school zone, and amenities best suited to their lifestyle. It

Poverty, Politics and Race (The View From Down Here)

is a bet that the amenities at the top of the list would not be a landfill, sewer plant, cell tower, power plant, or any intense commercial or industrial development.

Higher income, well-educated communities are almost always successful in mobilizing opposition to polluting, dangerous land uses being permitted in their neighborhoods. However, low-income residents are often either uninformed on the underlying health risks such facilities bring, or feel powerless against those with the influence and money to win support for their project. The poor feel they have very limited control over their environment because housing at affordable rental rates are generally located in sections of the community with lower property values.

And that is exactly the type location that local government officials zone for more intense, land uses. It provides the developer low cost land acquisition in an area with existing infrastructure to support the project. And the local government officials can feel a sense of accomplishment for attracting a major business interest that will contribute to the tax base, create new jobs, and improve the local economy.

Moreover, the government and business community have in the past developed a winning strategy to get low-income communities to vote against their own best interests. The argument that the polluting or incompatible development will create high paying jobs for the community, while assuring poor residents that there is no conclusive

Poverty, Politics and Race (The View From Down Here)

data to show environmental risks to health and safety even if not true has been used with some success in the past. The poor, hungry for opportunities to improve their financial circumstances, and without clear facts on risks to their family's health and safety, may be convinced that there are more benefits than disadvantages to support such projects.

Therefore, poor neighborhoods have become the path of least resistance for polluting industries, making the poor most often the victims of environmental injustice.

Widely reported, past environmental disasters have brought attention to the horrible results of such injustices, and created some environmental heroes along the way. Those cases also led to more stringent regulations to ensure communities, regardless of economic status, are protected.

One of those heroes is Lois Gibbs who is today a well known environmental activist, and also the founder of the Center for Health, Environment, and Justice in 1981. She is considered the mother of Superfund, a federal fund created with fees from chemical and oil corporation for cleanup of sites contaminated by those industries. However, she started out content with her life as a wife and mother caring for her family in their working class neighborhood.

In 1978 she learned her neighborhood was located adjacent to a 20,000 ton chemical waste

Poverty, Politics and Race (The View From Down Here)

dump resulting from decades of toxic waste disposal by Hooker Chemical Corporation, a subsidiary of Occidental Petroleum and its predecessor. It changed the course of her life.

The land where the dump was located was sold at public auction in 1920, and turned into a municipal and chemical disposal site. Once the site became full in 1953, it was covered over with dirt and later sold to the Board of Education for one dollar. The deed noted that chemical wastes were buried there. Not understanding the danger of building on such a site, the Board built the 99th Street Elementary School in 1954 that officially opened in 1955 to serve 400 students.

Housing development began in the area around the dump site in the 1950s. Though there was a warning of the chemical wastes dumped at the Love Canal site in the transfer deed when the School Board took possession of the property, no such warning was provided to families who bought homes in these new subdivisions; and there was no way residents could know of the danger without such a warning.

The Love Canal community was made up of blue collar workers with average incomes of $10,000-$25,000. By 1978 there were 800 single family residences, 240 low-income housing units, and the elementary school located on the old toxic waste dump. Over the period in which families were settling in the area between the 50s and the 70s there were regular complaints of odors and strange substances appearing in yards and on school

Poverty, Politics and Race (The View From Down Here)

grounds. The City would simply send a crew to cover the substance with soil, but did nothing to test the substance to determine its composition and whether it was harmful.

After years of complaints, the City finally authorized a study that was completed in 1976. The New York State Department of Health also conducted a health study in 1978 by collecting air and soil samples, resulting in an order to close the elementary school. Lois Gibbs had already launched a one-woman campaign demanding answers and action to address questions about the growing suspicion of contamination and health risks to residents.

She had repeatedly requested that her small son be transferred to a school outside the landfill area after learning the school was built on top of a toxic waste dump through news reports, with no success. Her activism led to the creation of the Love Canal Homeowners Association (LCHA) in 1978, as more and more residents joined her cause, with a membership of up to 500 families. Gibbs became increasingly concerned that there was a connection between the school's location on a toxic dump and her son's ongoing health problems.

Residents demanded that the government provide resources to evacuate the area, in addition to closing the school, to protect the health of those living in the area. It did not occur, however, until the state health study was completed and revealed the magnitude of damage to the health of children,

Poverty, Politics and Race (The View From Down Here)

pregnant women, and families in general from the poisons from that site.

The study found there was an unusually high rate of miscarriages (having increased by 300%), still births, crib deaths, nervous breakdowns, hyperactivity, epilepsy, and urinary tract disorders. Between 1974 and 1978, 56% of children born in the Love Canal area had birth defects, including children born with 3 ears, double rows of teeth, and high levels of mental retardation. Based on the cumulative results from the government's scientific and health studies, families were eventually evacuated from Love Canal, the school was closed, Occidental paid a $129 million settlement, the site was cleaned up. But there was no way to repair the damage done to the lives of the people who lived there.

The Love Canal disaster is epic among environmentalists, despite many other horrific disasters like the Three Mile Island nuclear-reactor accident in 1979 in Pennsylvania, the Exxon Valdez Oil Spill in Alaska in 1989, and most recently the Deepwater Horizon explosion and BP oil spill in the Gulf of Mexico in 2010. First, because of the determined citizens' activism under the courageous leadership of Lois Gibbs, the Love Canal environmental disaster led to the passage of the 1980 Comprehensive Environmental Response, Compensation, and Liability Act (CERCLA), better known as Superfund. Second, it introduced America to Lois Gibbs who has since made it her life's work to ensure other U.S. communities have the knowledge and support to protect themselves

Poverty, Politics and Race (The View From Down Here)

against environmental risks and hazards to human health that her community did not have.

Third, it demonstrated that without a vigilant public, sometimes elected leaders don't get it right. The City government permitted the construction of an elementary school on top of a known toxic waste dump, and housing development in an area contaminated by the poisons from the dump. The school board, though warned of the potential hazards in the deed transferring ownership of the landfill property, built an elementary school there and placed the health of innumerable children, school personnel, and families at risk. Fourth, it almost single handedly awakened Americans to the importance of the environmental justice movement in order to protect the public against such governmental failures in the future.

I had the honor of serving on the Superfund Reauthorization Advisory Committee, at the recommendation of then EPA Secretary Carol Browner to President Clinton, during my last term as Tallahassee Mayor. I was appointed as a local government representative on the Committee. It was an experience like none other in negotiating with people from divergent positions, as we tried to come to terms on recommendations to the Administration and Congress in reauthorizing the law. They were delicate, but determined negotiations between environmentalists, representatives of corporations seeking fewer and less costly restrictions for waste disposal or emissions, health agencies and local government

Poverty, Politics and Race (The View From Down Here)

officials responsible for balancing the business interest of corporations with health, safety and quality of life concerns of the public, and legal experts.

It was an equally awe-inspiring experience to serve on the Legal Environmental Assistance Foundation (LEAF) Board with Lois Gibbs. LEAF provided legal advocacy for low-income communities in Alabama, Georgia, and Florida in "David and Goliath" battles over policies and permits for polluting industries that could severely impact the quality of residents' lives. It, like many advocacy organizations for the poor, did not have a steady and reliable funding source for its legal assistance to low-income communities to match the well funded corporate and sometimes governmental attorneys on the other side of the issue. LEAF counted on governmental and foundation grants, as well as limited membership dues, to protect the poor from increased air, soil, and water pollution. When those sources dried up during the economic crisis that started in the early 2000s, an unfortunate result was that organizations like LEAF closed their doors, leaving many of these communities defenseless – in spite of LEAF's many documented successes.

It, then, falls to the Federal Environmental Protection Agency, departments of Environmental Protection in each state, local government planning, environmental and permitting agencies, and departments of public health to gives as much weight as possible to ensuring public health and safety as the competing economic interests of the

Poverty, Politics and Race (The View From Down Here)

community. There should not be a different value placed on the lives of residents whose homes have lower property values compared to those parts of communities with higher tax values. Nor should decisions impacting human safety and health be based on the money bags available for campaign donations or lobbying; but rather on balancing the interests to allow winners on both sides.

The Love Canal inspired CERCLA/Superfund and provided the federal structure to create regulations, monitor compliance, require and oversee clean up should a disaster occur. It required fees and monetary damages from polluters for a dedicated fund to support clean- up efforts.

The law authorized two kinds of responses, removal actions and remedial actions. Removal actions addressed localized risks like removal of abandoned drums of hazardous substances, or contaminated surface soils that create acute risks to human health and the environment from release of hazardous substances.

The law identifies the responsible party for the pollution, identifies and includes contaminated sites on the EPA National Priorities List (NPL) for clean up. It has the authority to require polluters to clean up their own sites. If they do not comply, they can be fined up to $25,000 per day for each day of non-compliance. Permits can also be denied for use of the site until it is brought into compliance.

CERCLA is known as Superfund because when the law was first passed by Congress it

Poverty, Politics and Race (The View From Down Here)

established a Trust Fund supported by taxes on petroleum products and chemicals to provide funding for clean up. The fund reached its peak in 1996 with $3.8 billion available for clean up. The taxes that supported the fund expired in 1995. The Republican Party gained control of both houses of Congress in January 1995 and refused to renew the taxes on the petroleum and chemical industries necessary for continued dollars for clean up to maintain the Trust Fund.

President Obama has as a goal to renew the tax. Without the trust fund "orphan" sites, those with no identified responsible party and that make up almost half the sites on the NPL, would have no source of funds for clean up. The Deep Water Horizon oil rig explosion resulting in the unfortunate death of oil rig workers and the BP Oil spill disaster in the Gulf of Mexico is the best example of why these taxes need to be renewed.

That spill destroyed the waters of the Gulf, caused immeasurable environmental damage, and crippled the economy of that coastal region for almost a year. There will likely be permanent damage to the coast and beaches of four states, marine life, birds, wildlife habitats, and coastal vegetation, even though the economies of the Gulf States seem to have bounced back. And there is no way to make up for the lives lost in the explosion, or the pain of the families who mourn the loss of their loved ones.

With the potential for that level of devastation and harm to human life and the

Poverty, Politics and Race (The View From Down Here)

environment being repeated, it seems a no brainer that a tax should be levied against the industries that are the most likely source of any future pollution. Further, it is important that low income communities have an opportunity to educate themselves to become their own best advocates, by understanding the risks involved. Instead of being fooled that environmental concerns are all about liberal tree huggers with a motive to drive off good paying jobs, local environmental justice workshops by churches, neighborhood associations, public health organizations, universities, and other organizations can provide low-income residents with the knowledge and tools to protect their communities against negative impacts of some governmental decisions.

There are options for siting polluting uses away from populated areas where there is the greatest potential for harm. State and local government must just have the will to design rational growth, zoning and permitting regulations that protect the health of its citizens and the environment, while at the same time achieving its economic development and job goals. The goal of environmental justice advocates is place a high value on the right of everyone to breathe clean air, to drink clean water, eat safe foods, and live in an environment free of hazards to health and safety.

Poverty, Politics and Race (The View From Down Here)

Chapter 10

The Survival of Public Education

Poverty, Politics and Race (The View From Down Here)

From the creation of the Department of Education in 1867 to the present, the federal government has recognized its role in ensuring access to a quality education for America's children, and later for post secondary education in 1890 with administrative support for land grant colleges and universities. In 1944 Congress passed the GI Bill making post secondary education accessible for veterans returning from World War II.

The 1958 National Defense Education Act provided greater emphasis and federal support for math, science, foreign languages, and vocational/technical training in the American education system. Congressional action beginning in the 1960's and throughout the 1970s introduced Title VI of the Civil Rights Act, and Title IX, Section 504 of the Rehabilitation Act that ensured that race, sex, and/or disability did not create a barrier to fair, equal access to education.

Children have been required by law to attend school since 1852 in all states in the U.S. The majority of these children have received their elementary and secondary education in public schools — supported by a combination of federal, state, and local funding. This was an era when teaching was almost universally viewed as a proud profession, widely supported by parents and the community. My teachers were my heroes and role models. It was because of teachers like Ms. Gregory and Ms. Coleman in Elementary School, and Ms. Hayes and Mr. Vann in High School, which I decided also to become a teacher.

Poverty, Politics and Race (The View From Down Here)

For 28 years, I was completely committed to that profession; and though I have not taught since 1998, I feel a real sense of joy and pride every time a young sheriff's deputy, lawyer, pharmacist, city employee, bank clerk, teacher or parent stops me on the street or in the market to remind me that I was their teacher many years ago as they eagerly update me on their lives and their successes. Like most teachers, I feel a great deal of pride in the accomplishments of the children I taught as if they were my own children. And at one point they were, for five days out of each week.

Like the teachers of my childhood, the teachers I had the pleasure of working with throughout my career cared deeply for the children they taught, worked hard, stayed late, and saw each child as an individual with unique talents and needs, while also teaching them to work as a team. Always, however, the success of the child was the joint responsibility of the home, the school, and the community. And the outcomes were most positive when all partners were actively engaged.

In the years since I left the classroom for another profession – leadership and advocacy for the poor – I have been shocked at the state of education, the disrespect for the ever demanding role of teachers, and the knee jerk, simplistic, political solutions to complex problems in our public schools that require accountability beyond the classroom. Over more recent years there has been too much focus given to bashing public schools, where most American children are educated.

Poverty, Politics and Race (The View From Down Here)

I was happy that I had made another career choice by the time then Governor Jeb Bush decided to model educational reform in Florida after his brother's, then Governor George W. Bush, plan to determine the worth of children and schools based solely on their test taking skills . In a column in the September 20, 2000 local newspaper – the Tallahassee Democrat – I expressed my concern over Governor Jeb Bush's plan to turn the Florida public school system into a testing factory using the Florida Comprehensive Assessment Test (FCAT) results to label schools with A-F grades. An excerpt follows.

"If children have had it drilled into them, with sample test after sample test, which multiple choice answer is more likely the correct one – is there any real learning going on? Accordingly to Dr. Merlin Langley, clinical psychologist in the Florida A&M University School of Social Work, there is – but not the kind of learning we should want for our children.

The term he uses to describe this 'teaching the test' phenomenon is operant conditioning; or shaping behavior through positive reinforcement or punishment. The punishment is a D or F ranking for the school and the loss of school funding for schools that need it most, and the retention of children based on a single test, in total disregard for the child's learning style or additional assessments for the child's performance throughout the year. In other words, a bad performance on test day could label a child a failure who may have performed satisfactorily throughout the year.

Poverty, Politics and Race (The View From Down Here)

Langley thinks, and I agree, that 'discovery learning' is a far more desirable approach to education. This is not learning by rote, but instead the teaching of critical thinking and problem solving. This type of learning has more meaning and relevance for the child, and provides other options for success in addition to test taking."

I further pointed out the heart wrenching impact so much concentration on the FCAT was having on our children. An excerpt from a "60 Minutes" broadcast included in my column shows a mother as she recounts her child's fear as the day of the test approached in his Texas school.

"His mother spoke of the terror he experienced. All her elementary school-aged child could think about was passing or failing the test, due to the government and school's complete emphasis on test scores to measure children's worth.

A Tallahassee Democrat editorial page cartoon showed a teacher saying to her class, "Welcome to the fifth grade. Please take out your Ritalin and your FCAT study books. We only have six short months 'til the test'. Let's save the school parades for school reform that works without traumatizing our children in the process."

Over time there was recognition by the State of Florida that other factors had to be considered besides the strict adherences to FCAT test results as the sole determinant for the fate of our children and the public school system. It is not a fair comparison to expect the same results from Title I

Poverty, Politics and Race (The View From Down Here)

School students. Many children come to school hungry. Others may lie awake all night due to violence in the home or neighborhood and arrive at school tired and sleepy. Some may have undetected deficiencies or needs like glasses, or hearing aids.

Or suppose on the one day, test day, on which the child's whole year in school would be judged, the student could not concentrate because of a mind numbing tooth or headache.

Just as detrimental as determining a child and school's success by one test was the plan by the Bush brothers to take much needed funding from public schools in order to fund private school vouchers. These vouchers were proposed to allow parents of children in under performing schools to choose private schools, paid for with public dollars. It was an incredibly short sighted approach to school improvement. My concerns were made clear in the following excerpt from another op-ed in the local newspaper.

"The Bush administration's opportunity scholarships, another name for private school vouchers, are of special concern to me. Giving vouchers to some students for private schools does absolutely nothing to improve the conditions of the schools they are leaving. If Governor Bush really wants to make a substantive and positive difference in the lives of children in schools ranked at the bottom, he might begin by looking with more depth at the real obstacles facing the schools in educating the students in their care. The children are not failing because of the performance bar and test

Poverty, Politics and Race (The View From Down Here)

score requirements. They are failing because they often start the race weighed down by such heavy baggage that it is impossible for schools to make up lost ground without a major commitment of additional resources.

Higher performance requirements are commendable, but will do no more than stereotype children and schools unless we also address the underlying cause of their poor performance. We will create environments in schools where all children can succeed when we finally recognize that families, schools, and communities must be seen as partners in this endeavor – equally responsible for our children's success and equally accountable for their failures."

The emergence of Charter Schools provided a different and more palatable option than school vouchers for private and religious schools – antithetical to America's promise of a quality public school education for all children. Since school vouchers actually reduce the funding for the school the student was leaving – this plan simply makes the school's job even more difficult by reducing resources available to educate all the other children. It always seemed so unfair and insensitive to the needs of the many children left at the "low performing" school to base reform around the child who receive the voucher, instead of seriously looking at best practices to improve the school so that the rest of the children will have the same opportunity for success as the child who received the voucher.

Poverty, Politics and Race (The View From Down Here)

Charter Schools were introduced as the next magic bullet for educational excellence. At first, as with private school vouchers, the government made no effort to create a level playing field from which to judge the public school against the new plans. The private or religious schools and charter schools receiving public funding through vouchers were not held to the same strict requirements. Nor were they required to provide documentation to the state that their schools produced better outcomes for the students.

Initially Charter Schools in Florida were introduced as the perfect public/private partnership because they assured the Legislature that private funding would be used for facilities or any other capital improvement. The per child or FTE funding, by way of the voucher, would be the only public funding requested. However, it was not long before these charter schools were before the Legislature and Governor with requests to compete for the limited Public Education Capital Outlay (PECO) funds for school facilities once they got their feet in the door. And they won.

The outcry by Public School advocates over Charter Schools getting all the benefits of public schools, without the same accountability requirements, led to changes in the charter structure. They now would be administered and fall under the policy guidelines of local school boards. In addition, they would be held to the same standards of accountability as other public schools – only with flexibility on program design and specialty.

Poverty, Politics and Race (The View From Down Here)

In the end, no special school is needed for educational improvement. Innovative best practices, with a keen eye for individual needs of the students, work in any school environment if there are dedicated school personnel, and adequate resources to address students' needs in a comprehensive manner.

I tested this theory with a juvenile justice grant funded project titled "Project Fresh Start", a gifted program for low-achievers. The program was based on the premise that 1.) All children have the ability to succeed in school; 2.) The right and left brain hemispheres translate and respond to information differently and therefore classroom experiences must be designed for a range of learning styles; 3.) Student expectations must be clear; 4.) Learning experiences must be interesting and interactive; 5.) The educational plan must recognize individual needs of the child beyond the academic and include opportunities to address them.

Project Fresh Start was a summer camp and after-school program during the school year — hosted at the Florida State University K-12 Research and Development School, but targeting troubled, low-achieving 4th and 5th graders referred by guidance counselors and teachers at four (4) local schools with the highest number of children on the free/reduced lunch program. The summer program was staffed by certified teachers and student counselors from both Florida State University and Florida A&M University, with a partnership agreement between the program and the FSU

Poverty, Politics and Race (The View From Down Here)

School of Psychology. Having the summer camp at the FSU location provided easy access to use of the campus pool and bowling lanes. Each of the six weeks of the program was designed around a weekly theme for each subject area – Math, Science, Language Arts, and Computer class. All academic classes were held when students were most alert and ready to learn, before the 12:00 lunch time. A teacher and teacher assistant/counselor created an adult to child ratio of 2 adults to every 8 children to allow students more opportunities for individual attention to their needs.

Recreational activities, Art, choral music, and mini field trips to the pool or campus bowling alley on Mondays through Thursday were scheduled in the afternoons. Some of the children were having these experiences for the first time in their lives. Thirty to 40 minutes each day was dedicated to quiet time reading.

The local public television station, WFSU, and book stores donated a wide range of books at every reading level, as well as comic books, coloring books, magazines. Even though the children were in grades 4 and 5 at their assigned schools, their actual reading levels ranged from 1st grade to 5th grade and above. As long as it was quiet time and everyone picked a book and read during this 30 minute period, it did not matter which book they read. At the end of each week, each child was allowed to pick a favorite book to take home to build an at-home reading library. A nutritious breakfast, lunch and afternoon snack were served each school day – recognizing that many of these children were

Poverty, Politics and Race (The View From Down Here)

from low-income, mostly single parent or grandmother-headed households with very limited incomes. We were well aware that the meals the children received in the program were likely the most nutritious meals they had during the summer, based on home visits.

Fridays, with boxed lunches, were field trip days based on the week's theme. For example, the field trip for the week dealing with weather and climate change was to the weather station at the Airport, a local TV station to observe a weather broadcast, picnic lunch, and a trip to the meteorology department on FSU's Campus.

At the beginning of the summer, many of the children tested the limits. However, consistency and quick consequences for violations of the rules – including quiet time at the classroom with a counselor instead of being able to go bowling, to the pool, or on that week's field trip with the rest of the group led to behavior modification, self control, and considerate, respectful conduct in short order. The two or three who repeatedly demonstrated behavior problems were referred to the FSU Psychology Department for the assignment of a counselor/mentor who met with the children both in the home, and on campus; and even on some weekends for a movie, one on one basketball, or just to talk.

By the end of the summer, there had been a complete transformation. Two important steps in the process were the way we started and ended the summer program. I met with each family in the

Poverty, Politics and Race (The View From Down Here)

home, upon receiving the referral from the school, to discuss the opportunity for the child to participate in an exciting summer camp, at no cost to the family; and personally received written approval from the parent, grandparent, or guardian, and child for camp enrollment. This initial visit provided an opportunity to build a rapport and begin to bond with the parent or guardian, and a chance to observe conditions in the home for clues not only to the child's need, but the needs of the whole family.

At the end of the summer program, the children knew we would be there to make sure that the gains they made during the summer continued during the school year through the project's after-school program set up at each of the four (4) schools. The After-School component of Project Fresh Start included homework/tutoring center for the first hour to ensure homework was completed before being allowed to attend Music, Arts and Crafts, Foreign Language, or Sports Centers.

As during the summer, Fridays were reserved for fun day or mini field trips. After-school snacks were provided. Parents and guardians were welcomed guests at the camp and on field trips. One child was suspended from the summer program for one day before pleading to be allowed to return, with promised compliance with program rules. The promise was kept.

Parent/child activities were sent home weekly to keep parents informed on educational activities, the curriculum, and to involve them with their child. The improvement in school

Poverty, Politics and Race (The View From Down Here)

performance and behavior was incredible at the end of the summer, and monitoring reports from teachers and school guidance counselors verified that the improvements continued during the school year. Unfortunately, the Florida Department of Juvenile Justice redirected prevention grant funds from which programs like Project Fresh Start were funded to detention programs like Boot Camps. And with no dedicated funding source, the program ended after just one year.

There, however, is nothing that was done through Project Fresh Start that could not be replicated in almost any school environment, if there is the recognition that the greater the learning gap, the greater the need will be for resources to help close that gap. There is no one size fits all in education. The individual needs and learning styles of children must be taken into account when designing classroom activities. And though there is some debate about small class sizes, it is essential that the adult to child ratio is such that no child feels left out or forgotten. Often children act out when they feel lost and are ashamed or don't know how to ask for help. When this goes on for a long time without intervention, those children generally become problems and drop out.

Therefore, school districts should provide an equitable and adequate level of support and resources to create learning environments that allow all children to succeed, or we can keep doing the same and accelerate our race to the bottom in educational achievement.

Poverty, Politics and Race (The View From Down Here)

There are many such programs being modeled in school districts throughout the U.S. These best practices simply need to be disseminated to provide opportunities for success for more children in America's system of public schools. The practice by states of siphoning off per student funding from public schools to create vouchers for charter, private, and faith-based schools is an insane approach. Schools with high numbers of low performing students need all the resources available to set up the kind of best practice learning laboratories to help children overcome a wide range of deficiencies. There should be a weighted formula that accounts for a greater funding allocation for schools with larger numbers of student with a higher level of needs.

I support public funding for charter schools when they are held to the same standards of accountability, with both charters and regular public schools allowed flexibility in designing model educational environments for student success, with a good monitoring and evaluation system. However, I see no good purpose in providing public funding for private or faith-based schools that are happy to take the public funding, but none of the conditions that come with the funds.

President Obama's administration's revisions to the No Child Left Behind Act demonstrate how this program has evolved since first introduced by President Bush at the national level. It was originally much more punitive in nature for children, teachers, and schools – with little recognition for the need to mitigate other risk

Poverty, Politics and Race (The View From Down Here)

factors that serve as barriers to children's school success. The revisions, with waivers to allow greater flexibility for states and school boards, permit the creation of educational laboratories to improve academic performance in more American schools. As noted previously, there is no one size fits all for every child or every school. Rigidly measuring success solely by FCAT and other state assessments has proven to be less effective.

As long as the federal and state governments resist the urge to stifle creativity in our schools, value the role of teachers and parents as true partners in this endeavor, there is great hope for the American public education system, and the future of our children, and the country.

Chapter 11

The Truth about Head Start

Poverty, Politics and Race (The View From Down Here)

A January 15, 2010 article by Dan Lips titled "Head Start: A $150 Billion Failure" was not supported by facts. Likewise, the 2012 John Stossel interview on Head Start with Lisa Snell, director of Education and child welfare for the Reason Foundation was full of inaccuracies. All three stated that Head Start was a failure and a 40 year waste of federal funds. Lisa Snell stated the federal government "spent $180 billion dollars on a program (Head Start) with zero advantage." Stossel enthusiastically supported Snell's position during the April 2012 televised interview. They based their conclusion on a 2010 report, commissioned by the U.S. Department of Health and Human Services/Department of Children and Families, titled, "Head Start Impact Study – Final Report". Snell, Stossel, and Lips incorrectly stated that this government report validates their claim that Head Start provides no positive impact on the children served because by 1st grade and 3rd grade, there seems to be no distinction between children who were enrolled in Head Start and those who were not. This is a well known trick. If you pick and choose passages from any source and quote them out of context, it is easy to make the words fit any narrative.

First, all three_ Snell, Stossel, and Lips_ are conservative voices for school choice, and private school vouchers who are also connected to equally conservative policy group; with no love for any of the safety net programs created in the 1960's to address the needs of the poor. Lips is a senior policy analyst for education with the Heritage Foundation, a think tank founded in 1973 to formulate and

Poverty, Politics and Race (The View From Down Here)

promote conservative public policy based on free enterprise, limited government, individual freedom, and traditional American values. Lisa Snell and the Reason Foundation, a libertarian research organization founded in 1968, opposed stimulus for education to prevent massive teacher layoffs in many states. Stossel, formerly a host on ABC's 20/20, now a FOX "fair and balanced" TV host, has a libertarian and free market point of view and fits well with the O'Reilly and Hannity gang at FOX News. Information on who these critics are gives context for their stated views.

More importantly, these three critics don't have a clue about Head Start's mission based on their critique. Nor did they understand the data and conclusions from the report. Either that or they deliberately misstated it for their own purposes. For that reason I have been surprised and a little disappointed that HHS has not pushed back more aggressively against these false interpretations of their report and Head Start. Since they chose not to do so, here is the truth about Head Start and the 20/20 report.

You must first be disassociated with the idea that Head Start was supposed to be the magic bullet for K-5 or K-12 education. You only need to read the purpose and mission for Head Start to understand that it is a comprehensive **school readiness** program for low income 3 and 4 year old children, and was never designed for the educational needs of 6, 7, or 8 year old children. It started in 1965, as an 8 week summer program, to correct deficiencies in the children's readiness for

Poverty, Politics and Race (The View From Down Here)

success in Kindergarten and to perform at the correct developmental age and on a level playing field with children from homes with greater resources.

However, recognizing that 8 weeks was not enough time to achieve that goal, Congress expanded Head Start in 1968 to a year-round program. When first created it was part of President Johnson's Great Society Campaign and was administered by the Office of Economic Opportunity's Community Action Program. It was later moved to the Department of Health, Education, and Welfare under the Nixon administration; and today is a program under the U.S. Department of Health and Human Services (HHS) and the Department of Children and Families (DCF).

The Head Start Act of 1981 had as its purpose to extend the authority for the appropriation of funds for comprehensive health, educational, nutritional, social and other services to economically disadvantaged children and families; to carry out these services to meet the needs of migrants with non-English language backgrounds, and Native American children, with the appropriate funding to meet those needs. In 1994 Congress created Early Head Start to extend these same comprehensive services to low-income children from birth to age 3 and their families.

A 1990 evaluation of Head Start, to which Lips referred in his critical analysis of the program, noted that Head Start participants lost their

Poverty, Politics and Race (The View From Down Here)

advantage by 3rd grade. The 2010 study indicated that by 1st grade, it became difficult to distinguish differences in the performance of Head Start children and those who did not attend Head Start Program. Based on that statement, long time critics of the program determined, therefore, that it must be a failure. They could not be more wrong, and for the following reasons.

1. Head Start was created to help poor children overcome deficits and barriers to **starting Kindergarten ready to learn** and at the appropriate developmental age. Nothing in the laws authorizing Head Start indicated that a goal of the program was to prepare children for 1st, 2nd, or 3rd grade. The child's Kindergarten is responsible for preparing him/her for 1st grade. Head Start has done its job when its graduates are performing at or above the appropriate developmental age for Kindergarten.
2. Due to extreme poverty, many children come to the Head Start program behind their chronological age by one to two years developmentally.
3. Comprehensive services are provided, that include readiness skills, health, dental, and special services to make up the lost ground by Kindergarten age.
4. Early Head Start, for children birth to 3 years old, has helped tremendously to erase the deficit and send children from that program to Head Start with developmental ages much closer to their chronological ages. However, all Head Start enrollees do not have access to Early Head Start.

Poverty, Politics and Race (The View From Down Here)

Therefore, these three Head Start critics are trying to judge the program by a standard it was never required to meet. Further, the federal government and tax payers get its money's worth with Head Start. The average annual per child expenditure for the Program I administered for 14 years was $9,524. That's $794 per month for each child or $26.46 per day. For that amount, these are the services Head Start participants received, at no cost to their families who must meet the 100% of poverty eligibility guideline.

Children receive the following early childhood development services.

- Basic concepts, such as numbers, letters, small words, colors, sizes, shapes, and development of gross and fine motor skills, social and daily living skills.
- Individualized education plans and instruction, if needed.
- Basic readiness activities through individual and group instruction.
- Developmental assessments and referrals.
- Group and individual recreation, dramatic play, and hands on art and science activities in full and part day centers, with an adult to child ratio of no more than 1:10.
- Field Trips
- Two hot meals daily for part and full day centers, plus morning and afternoon snacks for full day centers.

Special Services include:

Poverty, Politics and Race (The View From Down Here)

- Speech therapy – because children with language issues frequently do not perform at grade level, struggle with reading, and have difficulty understanding and expressing themselves. A stutter, untreated at an early age, can create a major barrier to a child's participation and performance throughout school.
- Psychological screenings help to identify behavioral concerns and a plan to address them for better social skills.
- Evaluations and examinations of enrollees diagnosed with suspected disabilities and ongoing therapy/treatment for enrollees diagnosed with disabilities; and counseling for parents of the children.
- Group and individual therapy.

Health and Dental Services include:

- Complete medical/dental screenings and examinations, follow ups and treatments.
- Needed immunizations
- Hearing and vision screenings, diagnostics, and appropriate treatments including glasses and hearing aids if needed.
- Health and nutrition education for children and their families.
- Daily brushing and flossing teeth after meals to create good oral care and health habits; including the provision of oral care kits.

Family Services are a major component of Head Start and requires a holistic approach to serving the child and family. Those services include:

Poverty, Politics and Race (The View From Down Here)

- At least 50% Parent participation as members of the Head Start Policy Council.
- GED and Adult Basic Education opportunities
- Workshops and parenting training sessions.
- Community Services handbook for each family, service referrals and direct assistance to families (transportation and individual counseling).

*Medicaid is used to cover expenses when possible.

The previous summary gives a detailed summary of services provided to children enrolled in the nine (9) Head Start centers under the agency I previously administered before retirement. The Head Start federal grant ensures that pre-school children throughout America have access to the help needed to start school ready to learn in spite of their financial circumstances.

Florida ranked 36 out of 50 states in per pupil public school funding, and spent an average of $9,084 per student compared to a national average of $10,297 – based on 2007-2008 data. New Jersey had the highest per student rate at $17,620. Taking into consideration the very wide range of services Head Start provides to the low-income children and families served, it has demonstrated excellent stewardship over the federal tax dollars received.

When compared to the average cost for center-based childcare in the U.S. at $11,666 annually ($972 monthly), our Florida Head Start program and Head Start programs nationally have continued to operate

Poverty, Politics and Race (The View From Down Here)

at a bargain for the public, while delivering high quality early childhood development services. These cost comparisons further debunk Snell, Lips, and Stossel's charge that Head Start wastes tax payer dollars and fails to achieve its mission.

The most current data available shows that 908,412 children were enrolled in Head Start in 2007. Children ages 3 and 4 were 87% of all children enrolled in Head Start. I seriously doubt if those low-income families served by the program would agree with Stossel and friends that Head Start has no value in improving their children's quality of life and giving them a good start toward educational success. A large percentage of Head Start parents were also able to complete college degrees, valuable job skill training, and jobs, secure in the quality of care provided to their children. That's important because while their children have been preparing for success in Kindergarten, parents have been preparing themselves with the skills and tools to overcome their financial barriers and gain economic stability.

Head Start, in addition to its 47 year history of excellent services to low-income children and their families in a fiscally sound manner, has maintained high quality program standards. Before retiring, it was an important accomplishment that all nine of the Agency's centers had been nationally accredited by the National Association for the Education of Young Children (NAEYC) for high quality early care standards. Every 5 years, the centers receive a site visit as part of the accreditation renewal process.

Poverty, Politics and Race (The View From Down Here)

More importantly, however, HHS requires that all Head Start Programs and centers receive an intensive, weeklong monitoring visit by a team of expert consultants to verify compliance with all applicable standards and regulations every three years. Any centers found in non compliance must correct all deficiencies within a specified, short time frame. If appropriate corrective action is not made where critical findings were reported, the program is defunded. In such cases, HHS advertises for proposals from other providers with capability to deliver the services to Head Start families and meet all applicable regulations. The intent is that continuity of services are to be maintained for Head Start families if there is a change in providers – even if an interim provider must be selected while a formal selection process is carried out.

Presidents, both Democratic and Republican, have supported the Head Start Program since a national panel of experts released its recommendation for a Head Start program in February 1965. The panel recognized that poverty robs children of resources and experiences important to their success in school. The report stated that "to be successful, the program must be comprehensive and involve activities generally associated with the fields of health, social services, and education". It also recommended that the program focus on both the needs of children and their families. Almost 50 years ago, it was clear that a combination of parenting, quality care and school readiness services, access to a variety of health and social services were absolutely necessary to give impoverished children a real chance at overcoming

Poverty, Politics and Race (The View From Down Here)

a multitude of barriers and achieve success when they start Kindergarten.

Head Start critics repeat half truths, distortions of the facts and misinformation for the simple reason that they do not support public funding for this program for the poor children, anymore than they support other important safety net programs for the America's poor. However, they have no such reservations against giving public funding to private or faith-based schools, subsidies to wealthy oil companies, and tax breaks to the wealthiest Americans.

Finally, let me quickly summarize the points in response to Head Start's critics. The first is the charges that Head Start funding should be terminated because a study indicated that by first to third grade the positive advantages of the program start to fade. Here's the point. Head Start's mission is to prepare poor 3 and 4 year old pre-school children to be developmentally ready for Kindergarten. It was never an expectation in 1965 or today that a program for toddlers and four year olds would do any more than the law states and is emphasized in the program's name_ to give poor children a head start toward success in Kindergarten.

Second, there is the charge that Head Start is a waste of tax dollars. Close to a million children benefited from the program in 2007, and made it possible for parents to improve their education, job training, and financial status and gain financial independence. All evidence shows that Head Start

Poverty, Politics and Race (The View From Down Here)

is one of the most closely monitored of the federal programs, with clear policies for defunding those that do not comply with standards and regulations. These programs have been doing the work for which they were created for 47 years; with the one I know best having received national accreditation for high quality. The cost per child is lower than the national average for childcare facilities that do not provide a fraction of the services received by Head Start participants. Annual external audits are required by all funders and centers that have been in continuous operation for 47 years are obviously doing something right.

With the hard work this program has been doing so well for almost five decades, it has earned its good reputation, funding, and even thanks.

Poverty, Politics and Race (The View From Down Here)

Chapter 12

Unions (Heroes of the Middle Class and Poor)

Poverty, Politics and Race (The View From Down Here)

Mention the words organized labor or labor union today and the response is barely disguised hostility among many Americans. This is quite a change from the historic beginning of organized labor in America. After all, unions are credited with setting in motion child labor laws, and the establishment of major worker reforms that included a federal minimum wage, benefits, overtime pay, the standard work day and work week, workers compensation, and work place health and safety laws. Collectively, these laws helped to establish America's middle class by creating a level of fair compensation for workers and pension benefits for retirees that have provided a pathway to prosperity for more Americans. Union membership was at its peak during these early days at 31.4 union members for every 100 non-agricultural worker.

We were reminded in 2011 of the historic achievements resulting from the labor movement when suddenly unions were on the verge of extinction when a new wave of elected leaders took control of governor's mansions and state legislatures. The Republican Party on steroids, under pressure from the Tea Party pushing the GOP to the extreme Right after the successful 2010 mid-term election, chose as its top priority the dismantling of public employee unions. With the public perception of unions having suffered over many years, Republican had been skillful in the past painting unionized employees as greedy, demanding, and an easy scapegoat for elected officials to blame for state budget problems that in reality were created by their own excesses.

Poverty, Politics and Race (The View From Down Here)

The new Wisconsin Governor, Scott Walker, had given no clue during his campaign of his animus for unions; and actually had the support of public safety employee unions in securing his victory. Therefore, when the Governor and the Republican-controlled Wisconsin Legislature launched its campaign to deny teachers collective bargaining rights and exempted police and firefighters, they expected an easy victory. It was the perfect example of a divide and conquer strategy. However, it did not work out quite that way.

The action by the Governor, instead of dividing union members, had the opposite effect. Feeling solidarity and the potential that these same leaders could just as easily turn on them next, unionized workers came together in one of the largest and most spontaneous demonstrations that I had seen since the Civil Rights movement in the 1960s. It was beautiful to witness average Americans choosing to stand up and fight for the principles in which they strongly believed, even there might be risks to their own personal well being.

It was clear that this battle between unions and state government in that state would have repercussions far beyond that Wisconsin, and quickly caught the attention of national media as crowds of peaceful demonstrators against the state's law rose to more than 100,000 at the peak. The Republican Party, with Governor Walker being one of its rising stars, also took notice and recognized this was a battle they could not afford to lose.

Poverty, Politics and Race (The View From Down Here)

The GOP was strongly in favor of Right-to-Work laws that limited the ability of unions to organize, recruit members, and collect union dues. The South was solidly Right-to-Work, and had been successful in severely weakening unions in that region of the United States. Of the fifty (50) states, twenty-three (23) were Right to Work states. Walker's union busting law limiting the collective bargaining rights of teachers was widely thought to be his first step toward a moving Wisconsin to the Right to Work column as well.

Other Republican state houses and governors were watching Wisconsin closely as a model they planned to follow if the Governor was successful. As predicted, Wisconsin Governor Scott Walker's bold action to strip public employees of collective bargaining rights, in effect since 1930, inspired other Republican governors to follow his lead. Governor Kasich of Ohio did not wait and launched a campaign against public employees' right to organize and collectively bargain the rights and conditions of their employment. He successfully moved his own union busting law, modeled after the Wisconsin law, through the Republican controlled Ohio Legislature.

Unions and their supporters responded quickly with rallies and protests similar to those in Wisconsin. Through a sustained movement that included unions, employees, their families, supporters from throughout the state, and contributions to their efforts from those who supported and sympathized with their plight throughout the U.S., workers in Wisconsin were

Poverty, Politics and Race (The View From Down Here)

able to mobilize the kind of mass support to collect a million signatures, double the number required, to force recall elections for the Governor and key Legislators. The election was successful in ending the political careers of two of the six legislators, but failed to unseat Governor Walker.

The national Republican Party, seeing the battle to recall one of its most prominent new Governors as one they had to win, pumped over $13 million from Super PACs and reliable Republican donors like the Koch brothers into Walker's campaign. Walker's fundraising was 670% more than his union supported opponent was able to raise; and they were, therefore, outmatched and lost the race. Seven major employee unions launched a court challenge in court against the law. The grounds for the challenge were that the law severely and without merit narrowed the employment terms that could be bargained by public employee unions, required unions to recertify each year by a majority of all members, while denying voluntary payroll deductions for dues.

Ohio Governor Kasich's law would have restricted collective bargaining rights for more than 350,000 teachers, police officers, state workers, and other unionized public sector employees. Rather than launching a recall campaign, as in Wisconsin, the **We Are Ohio Coalition** formed to oppose the law. The group kicked off a campaign to collect the 231,000 valid signatures required to place the law before the voters in a referendum on the November ballot. The group collected over 1.3 million signatures and got the attention of Republican state

Poverty, Politics and Race (The View From Down Here)

leaders. The Kasich law was defeated by a landslide of 61%, considered a true victory for working Americans.

In 2012, there was finally a ruling on the case brought by the Wisconsin unions in the District Court. The court upheld the state's ability to limit the issues to be collectively bargained, but ruled in favor of the unions on the other two issues. U.S. District Judge William M. Cohen included in his ruling the following rationale on the two issues in favor of the unions.

"So long as the state of Wisconsin continues to afford ordinary certification and dues deductions to mandatory public safety unions with sweeping bargaining rights, there is no rational basis to deny those rights to voluntary general unions with severely restricted bargaining rights."

I found the Judge's ruling interesting because while he acknowledged the disparity in the way the state was treating the teacher unions compared to other public employee unions, he only struck down two of the three areas of inequitable treatment. Even as he gave specific attention to the fact that the teacher union's rights were being "severely restricted" by the state while public safety unions were allowed "sweeping bargaining rights", he allowed that inequity to stand. Both sides, however, declared victory, while acknowledging disappointment in the part of the ruling in which they were unsuccessful, as the case moved to the 7th Circuit Court of Appeals.

Poverty, Politics and Race (The View From Down Here)

The Wisconsin and Ohio cases illustrate perfectly what can happen when power is so concentrated on one side of the political spectrum and there is not commitment to fair and equal treatment for all. Unions were generally considered by the Republican Party to be Democratic Party constituents; so it was no surprise that they became a convenient target of the GOP. With a crucial Presidential election looming, Republicans felt a strategy to weaken unions, a reliable source of campaign contributions and volunteers for progressive candidates, would also weaken the fundraising and ground campaign for Democrats in the upcoming 2012 presidential and Congressional elections. They recognized there had been a major decline in public perception of unions over the years and attempted to capitalize on it for political purposes.

From its high mark of 31.4 union members out of every 100 worker in 1947, union membership declined to 20.1% in 1983 – or 17.7 million union workers. By 2010 union membership had fallen to a 70 year low of 11.8%. The biggest decline has been in private sector membership at 6.9%. Among public sector unions, the membership has remained high at a 2011 rate of 37%. Blacks, denied membership in the early history of unions, today are more likely to be union members than White Americans and any other ethnic group or race.

The most recent union activity to shape public opinion and support is the Chicago teacher strike that began September 10, 2010. The School district insisted the impasse in contract

Poverty, Politics and Race (The View From Down Here)

negotiations was over union opposition to a slightly lower proposed pay increase to the average teacher salary of $76,000.

The Chicago Teachers Union countered that the unresolved issues were instead (1.) the requirement that 25% of a teacher's annual evaluation be based on student performance — including test scores; (2.) the terrible condition of public school facilities; (3.) the need for class sizes smaller than 35 to 50 students; (4.) better classroom resources, and (5.) the need for wrap around services to address holistically the problems their mostly low-income student population bring to the classroom. CTU insisted the compensation package was not the sticking point that led to the impasse, as widely reported in the media.

In addition they claimed the proposal from Jonah Edelman and Stand for Children, a national child advocacy group affiliated with the national Children's Defense Fund founded by Marian Wright Edelman, was the real sticking point in the negotiations. Jonah is the second son of CDF's founder, and obviously touched a nerve with the union when it was reported that he boasted about getting the school system to require a 75% majority vote of the full union membership before a strike could be called. CTU succeeded in getting a 90% vote from its members for the strike that began September 10, 2012.

Jonah Edelman apologized for comments made at the Aspen Institute, and added the following.

Poverty, Politics and Race (The View From Down Here)

"Stand for Children and I share a commitment with teachers and teachers union leaders to ensuring the most qualified individuals choose the teaching profession, that teachers have the preparation, tools, support, and school climate they need to do their best work."

Televised news reports and newspapers, however, continued to condemn teachers and the union for turning their backs on students and parents by choosing to strike. Several reports accused teachers of greed and total disregard for the well being of their mostly low-income students and their working poor parents.

It was evident that the media's sympathy was not with teachers, and helped to shape negative impressions about teachers and teacher unions. No such condemnation was directed at the school district or local government officials that could have worked harder to find common ground and avert the need for a strike. Negotiations in good faith mean both sides cannot lose sight of the big picture – providing opportunities for a quality education for all students.

As a retired 28-year educator, founder of Big Bend Stand for Children in the early 1990s, I closely relate to the heroic work and the challenges facing unions and unionized workers in today's environment; and at the same time, I have great respect for CDF and Stand for Children's long history of passionate advocacy on behalf of the nation's children. However, as a former union leader and a former city commissioner and Mayor, I

Poverty, Politics and Race (The View From Down Here)

have had seats on both sides of the table in collective bargaining sessions. Understanding that in most of these cases, there are good people on both sides with different approaches to the problem, in this case there did not seem to be an enemy; just a failure to communicate. The proposals from all parties seemed to have a common goal...a quality education for the children.

Further, since I am very familiar with the work of Stand for Children, I could not imagine the organization making a proposal that was counter to that goal. So I was eager to take a look at the recommendations influenced by Jonah Edelman and Stand for Children. The following are recommendations excerpted from the Illinois Senate Bill 7, passed with advocacy and support from Jonah Edelman and Stand for Children.

Those recommendations are as follows:

1. That teacher performance and qualifications serve as the primary determinant in teacher layoffs with seniority playing a secondary role.
2. Management has the unfettered right to hire teachers who best fit the needs of the school based on performance and qualifications — regardless of whether positions are filled through in-school promotions, in-district transfers, or new hires.
3. For tenure, teachers must receive two proficient or excellent performance evaluation ratings during the last three of a four year probationary period.

Poverty, Politics and Race (The View From Down Here)

4. New teachers who earn three excellent performance reviews in their first 3 years of a 4 year probationary period will be granted accelerated tenure in just 3 years.
5. Teachers can earn tenure portability when they move to another Illinois school district in just 2 years if they receive two excellent performance ratings in each of the first two years.
6. Teachers receiving two unsatisfactory ratings in seven years may be reviewed by the State Superintendent for revocation of certificate or professional development opportunities to help them improve.
7. Putting students' well being at the Center of Contract negotiations by requiring:

    - For an impasse in which mediation does not resolve issues, the unresolved issues will be made public.
    - Before a strike, a 90-day fact finding process, a 30-day notice period to the public, and a vote of 75% of the entire membership must be achieved.
    - Chicago Public Schools to have control over establishing the school day and year, with input by teachers through the negotiation process, though the impact of such decisions would be an issue for collective bargaining.
    - Surveys completed by students and teachers on the instructional climate of the school to assist the district and community in school improvement.

8. Streamline dismissal process giving school boards final dismissal authority after fact finding.

Poverty, Politics and Race (The View From Down Here)

9. The process involves a second evaluator for performance related dismissal.
10. For dismissals for cause or that are conduct related, the hearing officer's findings are binding with the School board determining if the conduct merits dismissals.
11. Narrows scope of cases to be determined or appealed in court.
12. And ensure strong school board oversight by requiring each member to complete at least four hours of training.

Though several requirements under the Bill give more control to school Boards and weaken control by unions to have those issues determined in collective bargaining, they are few and are within the purview of the Board's primary responsibility for appropriate management and oversight in maintaining a quality educational system. At the same time in areas dealing directly with teacher rights, supportive work environment, resources to achieve classroom goals for students, compensation and benefits, the Bill seems to leave in place collective bargaining rights while giving clarity to expectations for all stakeholders in ensuring a quality education for students.

Illinois Senate Bill 7 seemed to walk the fine line of raising the bar for public schools to promote school improvement, and at the same time, attempted to create real partnerships with teachers in achieving those goals, including incentives for excellence. Before reading the Bill, I was under the assumption that there would be draconian elements for which I was prepared to oppose. I was surprised

Poverty, Politics and Race (The View From Down Here)

to find instead a comprehensive, well reasoned plan for school improvement that actually looked at every facet of the school system for the purpose of establishing clear district wide expectations and the process to achieve them.

At the same time, the list of issues cited by the CTU had a great deal of validity. The news reports noted that the Chicago Public Schools student population was 85% free and reduced lunch, often from some of the most violent neighborhoods, in homes with few resources to support their educational needs, and more likely than not _ under educated, absent or uninvolved parents due to work schedules or because they do not feel welcome. For these children, the school is often a temporary escape from many stresses caused by their poverty. These children need far more than the educational preparation the school is meant to provide. No teacher, regardless of commitment and preparation, will be able to overcome the many challenges their students bring to school with them if there is not a recognition that schools must make resources available in schools serving high poverty populations to comprehensively address children's needs. Children can't concentrate on proficiency in math and science if their family is in crisis, drive by shootings and crime make their neighborhoods dangerous places, and their poverty leaves them hungry, utilities disconnected and no way to read homework, moving several times in a school year, with little stability in their lives.

Under those circumstances, it becomes completely unfair to judge teachers' performance

Poverty, Politics and Race (The View From Down Here)

based on test scores of students for whom the district does not provide the resources to make meaningful improvement. The Senate Bill seems to recognize that by basing one fourth of the rating on student performance generally, with test scores being just one of the factors to be taken into account, complete responsibility for student outcomes cannot be placed at the door of teachers. However, recognition is not enough. A plan to address the problem is required. And teachers are the best equipped, in conjunction with the families and the school district in identifying those needs and resources.

Both sides seem genuinely concerned about creating schools of excellence. And on first glance, these reasonable people should have been able to find a workable solution short of a strike. Strikes are very infrequent in all unionized professions. In recent history, until the Chicago teacher strike of 2012, the most memorable were the Writers Guild and the recent strike by the National Football League players. The fans were back to support the NFL games as soon as the strike ended. And even the celebrities, whose work was put on hold during the writers' strike, joined the lines and supported the Writers Guild strike.

It is, therefore, out of line to assume teachers or other unionized workers would call a strike without having seriously agonized over the short-term impact on the students, schools, or their profession compared to the long term gains for all concerned by taking a principled stand. The quality of life most of this century's middle-income

Poverty, Politics and Race (The View From Down Here)

Americans enjoy likely would not have been possible without two centuries of hard, courageous work and advocacy by labor unions.

The very difficult jobs of teachers, public safety workers and the many unionized workers who built our cities, towns, cars and most of the things we routinely take for granted like planes in the air and trains running on schedule, state workers and local public employees efficiently and silently keeping government services delivered smoothly deserve our support. And so do the unions that helped to create humane working environments for America's workers who have made this country the envy of many other countries in the world.

America would be greatly diminished as a nation without the labor laws and worker reforms over the past century credited to union activism in America.

Poverty, Politics and Race (The View From Down Here)

Chapter 13

Romney Campaign: A Violation of Trust

Poverty, Politics and Race (The View From Down Here)

Mitt Romney projected an air of entitlement throughout his 2012 campaign for President. Not the entitlement for which Romney, Ryan, and the Republican Party regularly accused the poor. His was created from a life of privilege and wealth in which everything came easy to him. Family connections, influence, and money had easily opened doors for him throughout his life.

I have no argument over Romney's wealth. My problem is that his easy existence lulled him into the misconception that life is that easy for everyone; and made him blind to the fact that many more barriers stand between middle and low-income Americans and their dreams. It was that blindness that made him oblivious that he had insulted his hosts and the bakery that provided cookies at a campaign event held at the home of supporters, when he turned up his nose and refused to taste the cookies when offered. The cookies were not of a type with which he was familiar. But even rich people are expected to demonstrate good manners and common courtesy to those who are kind enough to host them in their home. For Romney, the rules are for everyone else except the wealthiest 1% of Americans who float above the rest of us on their cloud of money and power.

That sense of entitlement was definitely on display when he and his campaign decided they would not release his tax returns, as almost every other President and general election presidential candidate has done since the Nixon era. These tax returns give insight into the candidate's past financial conduct, as a preview to what to expect in

Poverty, Politics and Race (The View From Down Here)

the conduct of America's business. Romney finally relented, under pressure, and agreed to release only his 2010 tax return and an estimate for 2011, not the actual return. The campaign stubbornly ignored calls for more returns and left many wondering what this guy was hiding.

By comparison, below is a list of past Presidents, and the number of returns they released to the public, as proof that the expectation for Romney was no different than the standard set by past candidates seeking election to the office of President of the United States.

- President Obama released 12 years of returns, and Vice President Biden released 14.
- Both President George W. Bush and Vice President Cheney released 8 returns.
- President Clinton released 8 returns.
- President Reagan released 6.
- Presidents Carter and H. W. Bush each released 3.
- Even President Richard Nixon, "Tricky Dick", released 4.

Yet, Romney felt obligated to release only one actual return, even though the call for Romney to be transparent and release more returns had come from Republicans and Democrats, alike. The results of an August 2012 poll revealed that 63% of all Americans, 64% of males, 63% of women, and 81% of non-white Americans polled agreed that Romney should release more tax returns. The Romneys felt very put upon that they were not being allowed to unilaterally set the rules for the presidential

Poverty, Politics and Race (The View From Down Here)

campaign. Mrs. Romney, in an interview with Natalie Morales at NBC Rock Center, became irritated when the subject was broached.

Natalie noted, "A lot of people still are asking why not be transparent and release more than the 2010 (tax return), and the estimate for 2011. Should you not be questioned about your finances?" Mrs. Romney responded, "We have been very transparent to what's legally required of us, but the more we release, the more we get attacked. The more we get questioned, the more we get pushed."

However, the inquiries surrounding the one return Romney released were very legitimate, based on some questionable financial decisions that the return brought to light. They included the fact that Romney paid a very low tax rate of 13% compared to the much higher rate paid by middle income Americans who earn a fraction of Romney's income. It also showed that large amounts of his earnings have been vacationing in the Cayman Islands and in Swiss Bank accounts to avoid paying more taxes in the U.S.

So not only has he been outsourcing American jobs, he had been outsourcing his American made money, as well. Both actions are legal, but again presents an image of privilege as his running mate Paul Ryan introduced a House budget that pours even more money into the coffers of the Romneys and the super rich for their off shore accounts. Romney was a candidate focused like a laser on lowering the tax rates and eliminating

Poverty, Politics and Race (The View From Down Here)

loopholes for the rich, if elected in 2012. At the same time he recommended major tax increases for middle income Americans, while cutting the heart out of the safety net for the poor. Middle income families have few deductions to lower their tax burden, mortgage interest and exemptions for household members and found it hard to understand the desperation by Romney to hide as much money as possible and avoid paying taxes to the government he was seeking to lead.

Ryan's House budget proposed reducing the tax rate on the wealthy from the already low 35% Bush rate to a 25% maximum rate, placing the burden on the backs of middle income families and the poor. Republicans justified throwing more cash at the wealthy because they were the "job creators". However, these same wealthy corporations paid the lowest tax rate in decades under the Bush administration as American jobs disappeared in record numbers and shipped overseas. So I guess in that sense the Romney/ Ryan team was correct. They were job creators. The jobs were just being created in countries that did not include the U.S.

Under the Bush administration, jobs were probably among our biggest exports, at huge profits to these corporations, but little benefit to the American people. The GOP refused to acknowledge that these wealthy corporations were already earning record profits while the rest of America suffered.

Under President Clinton, at a higher 39% maximum tax rate for millionaires and billionaires,

Poverty, Politics and Race (The View From Down Here)

America experienced great prosperity, low unemployment rates, and real growth in the country's middle class. Clinton's economic policies were so successful that he was able to hand over an estimated $230 billion budget surplus to George Bush as he began his term as President, and reduced the deficit by $1.7 trillion based on projections.

Bush quickly reintroduced the trickle down financial policies of past Republican administrations, squandered the huge surplus from the Clinton administration, brought the American economy to the brink of disaster, then handed the country over to President Obama in January 2009 with the economy on life support and the nation's top financial institutions imploding. Bush era deregulation facilitated the risky behavior and greed that nearly toppled the U.S. economy. Mitt Romney and Bain Capital, for which Mitt was CEO, were major beneficiaries of this era of corporate excess. And though, during that eight years, these corporations were walking away with boatloads of profit, these "job creators" did not create American jobs. Instead, they laid off American workers, closed plants, and shipped the jobs to countries where they had access to labor at almost slave wages to further increase their profit margins.

Romney and Bain were among the leaders in outsourcing American jobs while closing companies and laying off workers in this country. Bush era deregulation made it easier to do so. These corporations were able to move jobs to countries that included China, India, and Mexico and

Poverty, Politics and Race (The View From Down Here)

tremendously increase their profits by paying wages as low as 60 cents per hour and no benefits. Unlike in the U.S., there were no environmental, workplace safety, or labor laws to protect the worker. The companies were, therefore, allowed to require very long work days and pay no overtime or benefits, in addition to paying wages so low it was almost criminal.

Then, these companies were allowed to benefit further from their horrible business practices that caused great damage to the American economy by importing the goods produced under these circumstances back to America, with no real penalties and at prices that undercut products from American companies. Basically, the regulations supported by Romney and Congressional Republicans not only encouraged the outsourcing of American jobs, but rewarded companies for doing so.

That's why the Republican argument that a capitalist like Romney is better able to deal with the nation's economy is so puzzling to me. First, it was the bad judgment and risky behavior of these wealthy business people that caused most of our economic problems. And, second, government does not have the luxury, nor should it, to simply shut down major functions of the federal government created to serve an important public need, and buy on-the-cheap in another country as these capitalists do when it serves their profit interests.

A President can't just look at the bottom line and has to understand that there are completely

Poverty, Politics and Race (The View From Down Here)

different objectives involved in the efficient delivery of governmental services than running a business. For one, the overriding goal in government is not to determine the worth of a governmental agency by the amount of profit it makes; but rather by the public need. Otherwise, as some Republicans would like, FEMA would be out of business. Further, almost every governmental experiment with privatization of government services to for-profit companies has ended badly; costing more than if the work had been done by public employees. The only exceptions have been when special waivers were provided to the private companies that were not available to government employees.

It is that history that made many Americans feel they needed to know more about the people seeking to control the purse strings of our country. I never understood why the Romneys found it so unfair that they were expected to follow the same rules as other candidates; particularly since Romney had no qualms about producing 23 years of tax returns to McCain in 2008 when he was under consideration as John McCain's Vice Presidential running mate

He, also, showed he understood the importance of reviewing multiple tax returns when considering his own 2012 running mate. Ryan admits he was required to submit several tax returns, clearly more than one or two, to the Romney campaign for the vetting process. Based on the 23 returns Romney gave willingly to McCain, and the several returns Romney required of Paul Ryan, he did not even follow the standards he

Poverty, Politics and Race (The View From Down Here)

required of others in his own run for President. And his continued refusal to release at a minimum the number he required of his Vice Presidential candidate, showed a disdain for the American public and the worst display of entitlement by any candidate in recent history.

Further, a look back at Romney's history in politics reveals a deep seated dishonesty, as well.

At the time Romney announced he was a candidate for Governor of Massachusetts in 2001, he was claiming his home in Park City, Utah as his primary residence. This presented a problem because Massachusetts' law required a candidate to be a resident of the state for seven consecutive years before declaring as a candidate to legally qualify to run for office. Romney had moved to Utah to run the Olympics in 1999. He listed his home there as his primary residence on his tax filings. Between 1999 and 2000 he received $54,000 in tax benefits as a resident of Utah. At the same time, he was claiming his home in Massachusetts as his part-time residence.

When Democrats in Massachusetts challenged him to release his tax returns to prove his residency and eligibility when he decided to run for Governor in that state, he refused and stubbornly held to that position until forced to come clean. He had to finally admit that according to his homestead filing and tax records, he was not a full time resident of Massachusetts, but a resident of Utah. After the fact, he retroactively revised his returns to change his residency status from Utah to

Poverty, Politics and Race (The View From Down Here)

Massachusetts, and repaid the tax benefit he had received by claiming Utah as his primary residence on his 1999 and 2000 tax returns.

Had an average American with less wealth and influence than Romney pulled a trick like that, they would have likely been charged with tax fraud and booted off the ticket as the Republican gubernatorial candidate. But for Romney, the fix was in and a Republican controlled elections Board accepted his retroactively corrected Massachusetts residency, and qualified him to run for Governor.

Likewise, Romney came under fire for Bain Capital, for which he owned 100% of the company's shares based on 2002 documents. Bain took over companies, put them out of business, laid off workers, then walked away with pockets full of cash at the expense of workers and the community's economy. Instead of accepting responsibility for his company's business practices, he denied any involvement in the company.

This time, he claimed residency in Utah, and that he had resigned his position as CEO of Bain Capital to devote 100% of his time and energy to running the Olympics beginning in 1999. As has become clear, Romney changes the story line to fit whatever lie he wants the public to believe at the time. When smart reporters found and released, to the public, documents showing that he continued to be listed on all Bain Capital documents as CEO, attended meetings, and continued to approve and sign company documents during this period, he retroactively resigned as CEO years after the fact.

Poverty, Politics and Race (The View From Down Here)

Romney has a long history of rewriting the facts to fit whatever narrative he chooses to put forth.

In this case, however, if he was not CEO at the time he was signing company documents, wouldn't those documents be considered null and void? And doesn't this create some liability for Bain Capital in having had an unauthorized person making important decisions, approving, and signing off on important company business? In the past, many in the media have laughed at Romney's "Etch-A-Sketch" approach to the truth; but it seems to have worked for him so far.

Basically, Romney has suffered none of the consequences average Americans would have suffered for conduct that is consistently bad, dishonest, and possibly illegal. The man has proven over and over again that his political ambitions override any other values or considerations. He has left the impression that he is an empty suit, with no inner core, values, or true beliefs; willing to say or do anything if it would move him closer to his goal of political dominance to match his wealth. During the 2012 presidential campaign, he had been on every side of every issue, and seemed unfazed by his lack of integrity.

Here's the Romney "Hit Parade". He was first against and now for the flat tax as later proposed by his Republican colleagues under a simplified tax code. When campaigning for Governor in Massachusetts in 2002 he supported abortion rights or a woman's right to choose. As a presidential candidate, in a National Journal

Poverty, Politics and Race (The View From Down Here)

article, he stated, "If I have the opportunity to serve as our nation's next president, I commit to doing everything in my power to cultivate, promote, and support a culture of life in America." He went on to say he supported overturning Roe v. Wade and defunding Planned Parenthood, a major source of women's health services with only about 3% related to abortion.

At one time he praised "Don't Ask, Don't Tell" as a good first step toward gays and lesbians being able to serve openly in the military. He later opposed President Obama's action to eliminate the policy and allow these courageous soldiers to serve openly. He supported contraception until he needed to prove his right wing credentials, and endorsed the GOP Personhood Amendment to state constitutions, and the proposed amendment to the U.S. Constitution that would prohibit abortions even in cases of rape and incest. The Personhood amendment took it farther and in some cases even prohibited contraception, taking away a woman's right to plan when she is ready for pregnancy and motherhood. In the end, this measure proved too extreme even for one of the most conservative states in the south, and the Mississippi ballot initiative lost by a vote of 55%.

As Romney prepared for the Republican Convention in Tampa, he revised his position again and stated he was opposed to abortion, except in cases of rape, incest, or the life of the mother. Yet, he vowed support for the platform adopted at the Convention that excluded those exceptions and strongly supported the personhood language, co-

Poverty, Politics and Race (The View From Down Here)

sponsored by his running mate that even prohibited contraception. It made me dizzy trying to keep up with his regularly changing positions.

The biggest flip flop of all, though, was on healthcare reform. As governor of Massachusetts, Romney passed the most sweeping healthcare reform package in the nation. In his book, No Apology, he proudly stated, "We can accomplish the same thing for everyone in the country". Then when President Obama introduced the Affordable Care Act, a plan designed to be almost a mirror image of the Massachusetts plan, making healthcare affordable for almost 50 million uninsured Americans, Romney had a change of heart. Suddenly the plan he created for Massachusetts was a government takeover when President Obama sought to make healthcare accessible and affordable to all Americans.

What could have possibly happened to turn him against his biggest accomplishment as Governor of Massachusetts? Obviously to gain the Republican nomination and hold on to the support of a party fractured by the Tea Party, Romney became adept at blowing whichever dog whistle necessary to maintain the support of the rabid right wing of the party.

He has proven to be ambitious, empty of any real concern for the American people, and also a bit dishonest. It was absolutely incredible that a person this empty of character traits needed for the job was in a dead heat with President Obama – an intelligent, confident and skilled leader. Romney

Poverty, Politics and Race (The View From Down Here)

had no real connection to average Americans, while Obama had proven himself through accomplishments ranging from saving the economy from the abyss, a rebirth for the auto industry, healthcare accessible to all Americans, and real strength in foreign policy throughout his first four years in office.

Add to all the other deficiencies, Romney's disastrous foreign policy trip, and it becomes impossible to understand how voters could have been evenly split in their support for the President and Romney within a couple of weeks of Election Day.

Poll after poll showed very few Americans liked Romney, and even fewer of them trusted him to care about their needs as President. And we all know by now that there was no position Romney has ever held that he was not willing to change for political expediency. Yet, Mitt wanted America to just trust him and felt it was unnecessary to show why he was deserving of the trust.

However, in the end, nothing in his pattern of lies, deceptions, and glorified self promotion made him a leader most Americans were willing to trust with the keys to the White House and the nation's bank account.

Chapter 14

President Obama – Breaking Down Barriers

Poverty, Politics and Race (The View From Down Here)

It would be difficult to write about poverty, politics, and race without including a chapter on a man whose life speaks volumes on all three. Obama was born in Hawaii, and spent most of his childhood between Hawaii, Samoa, and Kansas, the birth place of his mother. America's 44th President grew up in a single parent household, but with the support and nurture of his maternal grandparents. The humble manner in which Obama started his life did not slow his momentum toward a truly distinguished future. He was elected President of the Harvard Law Review, graduated with a Harvard Law degree, met and married an equally stellar Harvard Law School graduate Michelle (Robinson) Obama, and worked for the poor and downtrodden as a community organizer before deciding on a political career. His life until then gave him the real world experience and values that served him so well as President.

Obama has been beating the odds and making believers out of those who gave him no chance to win for most of his life. When as a fairly new U.S. Senator, he announced his intent in 2007 to run for President of the United States, few took him very seriously. At the time, I was a staunch Hillary Clinton supporter, having been among President Bill Clinton and First Lady Hillary Clinton's most fierce defenders throughout the Clinton era.

But this smart as a whip, wise beyond his years, good looking, well spoken, and cool under pressure young man, Obama, caught my attention. And at some point in late summer 2007, my

Poverty, Politics and Race (The View From Down Here)

maternal instincts took over and I began worrying and praying for his well being and success; and made the decision that he needed my support more than Hillary. I also concluded that there would likely not be another candidate like Obama in my lifetime, with the perfect combination of qualities to become the first Black U.S. President.

By September 2007, I had sent my first $200 Obama campaign contribution_ a lot for a social service agency director_ and set out to convince my husband and friends to join me in supporting this extraordinary young man. Converts were slow. Most Black Americans, though impressed with Obama, thought he did not have a chance in heaven or hell in capturing the Democratic nomination and wanted to back the most likely winner, Hillary.

Blacks were skeptical that any Black man could win wide enough White support, based on this country's history. Then what was thought to be impossible happened. Obama won the Iowa caucus in a predominantly White state in January 2008. It suddenly became much easier to recruit Obama supporters. By February 2008, my husband and I were so sure that Senator Barack Obama would be the next American President that we were already planning our trip to Washington for his January 20, 2009 inauguration.

A year later several members of our family traveled from Tallahassee, Birmingham, and Atlanta to join us and family in Maryland to be witnesses to history on that frigid January day as

Poverty, Politics and Race (The View From Down Here)

Barack Obama was sworn in by Chief Justice Roberts as the 44th President of the United States.

As he was being sworn in, a small group of top Republican leaders were meeting to plot a strategy to deny the new President a second term before the first had even begun. They started by denying and delaying Senate confirmation of his cabinet appointments, making it difficult for the new President to organize his team for the major challenges confronting his administration. The most difficult of which was the fiscal mess former President George W. Bush had left behind. The country was in a deep recession, beyond anything President Obama could have imagined; worse than anything since the Great Depression, with a monthly job loss of almost 800,000, and America's major financial institutions and Wall Street teetering on the brink of disaster. And despite dire predictions and the worst acts of obstruction in recent history by Republicans, Obama presided over an Executive Branch with more major achievements in a first term than any President since Franklin Roosevelt.

When Ann Romney spoke of hers and Mitt Romney's difficulties as they began their married life in a basement flat, having their meals on an ironing board, she neglected to say both she and Mitt had wealthy parents and, therefore, they lived that way by choice. Low-income Americans do not have the choice of a backup financial support system from well-heeled parents. They, instead, need the safety net that government provides; and that the Romney/Ryan team was determined to

Poverty, Politics and Race (The View From Down Here)

eliminate. When Mitt told young people if they needed money for college, get a loan from their parents, it demonstrated his lack of connection to real families who need President Obama's increased Pell Grants for that bridge to higher education, and careers.

The fact that both President and First Lady Obama were not able to pay off their own student loans until recently gave them the real life experience and authenticity to relate to all Americans, even as their income has risen to match those in the top 2% income bracket. The First Lady and the President have proven their deep concern and commitment to average low-income and middle income Americans through their fight for veterans and their families, small business, American consumers, and civil and citizenship rights of all Americans.

President Obama has demonstrated that commitment with a record of accomplishments in his first 4-year term that is unmatched by any recent U.S. President. His accomplishments total 200, and include the following among his major first term accomplishments.

1. The Lilly Ledbetter Act to require equal pay for women performing the same job as their male co-workers.
2. The American Recovery and Reinvestment Act (ARRA) stimulated the U.S. economy with jobs in the construction industry through Weatherization Programs for the poor, elderly, and disabled, small business credits, funds to

Poverty, Politics and Race (The View From Down Here)

retain jobs for teachers, police officers, and other public sector employees; job training and job creation which led to 3.3 million jobs.
3. The Bailout of the Auto Industry, opposed by the GOP and Romney who recommended "Let Detroit Go Bankrupt", not only saved General Motors and Chrysler from bankruptcy, but restored them to top status as auto manufacturers and created 1.1 million jobs.
4. Mortgage Foreclosure prevention funding.
5. The Affordable Care Act that provides access to healthcare for all Americans, extends the life of the Medicare Program by 8 years, requires Insurance companies to provide healthcare premiums for women equal to the lower rates for men, access to preventive care, expands services under Medicaid, removes pre-existing conditions as reason to deny coverage, and creates community health centers for more accessible, quality health services.
6. Ended Don't Ask Don't Tell that unfairly discriminated against Gay soldiers who courageously serve and defend our country.
7. Ended the Iraq war and brought our brave troops home.
8. Credit Card Accountability, Responsibility and Disclosure Act (CARD) to protect consumers from unfair, predatory or deceptive credit practices.
9. Strong Support for Veterans Affairs and expanded health services including mental health, the G.I. Bill for more educational opportunities for veterans, increased support for military families, job training and small business incentives to hire veterans, and

Poverty, Politics and Race (The View From Down Here)

housing to reduce or eliminate homelessness by veterans.
10. Homeless Prevention and Rapid Re-housing Program Grant to states to prevent homelessness and intervene to place homeless families in housing with a jobs component for economic stability.
11. Fraud Enforcement and Recovery Act that provided federal authority to investigate and prosecute the kind of fraud that led America into a recession and the meltdown of the U.S. economy in the closing days of the Bush administration.
12. Executive Order banning torture.
13. The capture and killing of Osama Bin Laden, responsible for the worst act of terrorism on American soil in our history.
14. Restored America's tattered international relations, and its reputation as the leader of the free world.
15. Stitched the gaping wound left by George Bush in America's economy that was bleeding almost 800,000 jobs per month on the day Obama was inaugurated.
16. More than doubled the rate of growth in the stock market, with the Dow going from 6000 to 13,000.

And while Mitt Romney presided over a company that was acquiring and bankrupting American companies, and outsourcing American jobs, President Obama was creating his creating his **Blueprint for an America Built to Last**. In it he proposed a reform package to support American

Poverty, Politics and Race (The View From Down Here)

businesses and jobs, and focused on discouraging the outsourcing of jobs. The major elements of his proposal were the following.

First, he would remove tax deductions for businesses that shut down operations here and outsourced jobs to another country. He also proposed the closing of loopholes that allowed these businesses to shift profits from their companies in the U.S. to their overseas operations to bypass tax obligations in America. Currently, a company closing its American plant to move operations overseas can get tax a tax deduction up to $350,000 for expenses of incurred of $1 million for the overseas move. Obama would eliminate that deduction and instead provide a 20% income tax credit worth $200,000 for companies moving businesses back to the U.S. to offset their costs.

Second, the President proposed the creation of a new Manufacturing Communities Tax Credit to help finance projects in communities that had suffered major job losses, such as the closing of a military base or a major manufacturing company for which the community that had been a major employer in the community. Third, he proposed temporary tax credits to encourage domestic clean energy manufacturing here in our country. Current subsidies to oil companies for oil production would be eliminated, and those dollars would be redirected to clean energy manufacturing activities. At the same time, the President also submitted proposals to Congress for major corporate tax reform. Under the proposal, he would require companies to pay a minimum tax for profits and jobs overseas, and

Poverty, Politics and Race (The View From Down Here)

those dollars to cut taxes for American manufacturers.

In addition, the President has proven to be a model for moral and ethical standards of conduct as a husband, father, and our President. He has been the complete package – supremely intelligent, and classy.

Therefore, it defies reason that a completely vacuous Mitt Romney ran neck and neck with Obama in polls throughout most of the 2012 Presidential election. Romney proved himself a complete "empty suit" with his disastrous campaign trip abroad, his absolute lack of understanding that the President represents all Americans not just the rich who look and act like him, his sense of entitlement that rules are for others, not him; and his lack of inner commitment to anything or anyone except his own ambitions.

Yet despite his many successes, this President has had to endure constant obstruction, lies, racism and hate beyond anything all other presidents had to deal with. And he has dealt with all of it with such intelligence, calm and grace that we should all be proud.

The day after the very successful 2012 Democratic National Convention, Delaware Attorney General Beau Biden _ son of Vice President Biden _ appeared on Morning Joe. Asked his opinion on the sharp division between Republicans and Democrats in Congress and his father's sharp criticism of the GOP at the

Poverty, Politics and Race (The View From Down Here)

Convention, Beau reminded the show panel of the collegial relationships that existed years ago when his father was in Congress, even among those with whom he strongly disagreed on issues. He added that his father maintained close working relations with Jesse Helms and Strom Thurmond, who were among the most conservative Republicans in Congress and representatives of one of the most racist era in our history.

Mika immediately asked, "Do you think your Dad can help the President to do that?" – implying that the hateful behavior of Republicans toward President Obama somehow was his fault. It was one of the most naïve questions, and as a Black woman, I was insulted by her willingness to excuse the horrible GOP behavior and instead blame the target of the vitriol for the discord in today's politics. It was as though Mika had been out to lunch for the past 4 years. Each of the show's commentators were very aware of the President's repeated attempts during the first 3 years of his term to work with the GOP and broker a compromise on much needed programs to repair America's economy. Every attempt was met with unanimous opposition by the GOP; even by Republicans considered in the past to be rational, moderate, and more interested in doing well for their constituents like Congresswoman Snowe, than towing the Party line for the most rigidly conservative Republican Party in decades.

Even when Obama angered his Democratic base in his determination to broker bipartisan agreement on issues, the response by Republican members of Congress was the same. On the

Poverty, Politics and Race (The View From Down Here)

negotiation to raise the debt ceiling, which before the Boehner led House of Representative was normal Congressional business, every time Obama and the Democrats thought they had a deal with Boehner and the Republican House, Canter and the Tea Party wing of the House rejected the deal and insisted on the Republican far right position. They either did not know the definition of compromise, or more likely just wanted to stick it to Obama; and did not care if the American people went down with him.

Senator McConnell proudly and publicly proclaimed that the Republican strategy was to deny Obama any success to ensure he would be a one-term President. When they refused to act on raising the debt limit until America's credit rating was downgraded, it became clear that they had made the calculated decision that the GOP's political future was more important than their obligation to the country, the American people, and the American and international economy. The Republican Party had become bullies who were willing to hold the whole country hostage.

President Obama's American Jobs Act would have created close to a million jobs for teachers, veterans, public safety workers, and the construction industry with a $50 billion investment in transportation infrastructure, $25 billion modernizing schools, and $15 billion rehabilitating and refurbishing hundreds of thousands of vacant and foreclosed homes and businesses to stabilize neighborhoods, payroll tax cuts, the temporary

Poverty, Politics and Race (The View From Down Here)

elimination of employer payroll taxes, and a wide variety of programs to support small business.

Everyone on Morning Joe and every other political commentator or journalist knew exactly what happened to the Jobs Act. It has been stalled in the U.S. House of Representatives for a year with no plans by Speaker Boehner to bring it to the floor for a vote, true to McConnell's word. Every attempt to forge a working relationship with Congressional Republicans by President Obama has been met with unanimous rejection. At one point the constant rejections of the President became insulting, disrespectful, humiliating, and made Democrats demand that he accept it was a lost cause and fight back. When in 2012 the President did just that, Democrats were happy, but thought he might have waited too late.

Yet, Mika didn't ask Beau Biden the correct question _ "What would it take to get Republicans to put politics aside and do what is right for America?" No one called these Republicans to account for their abuse of power and disregard for their duties to the country; but instead continued to allow the spin to go unchallenged that the President had refused or did not have the skills necessary to forge relationships with his rivals for the good of the country.

When Joe Scarborough noted that he saw a bus at the 2012 Democratic Convention with a banner that read, "We won't let you disrespect our President", it expressed the reason a summer 2012 poll showed 94% of African-Americans supported

Poverty, Politics and Race (The View From Down Here)

Obama over Romney for President. There is a real anger among Black Americans over the way the Republicans, and the predominant White media give the President none of the well-deserved credit for his hard won accomplishments under the most difficult circumstances; but are quick to hold him accountable for everything that is wrong in the country and Washington.

During the same Morning Joe Show, Joe, Mika, Jeff Greenfield, Chuck Todd, and Willie Guise discussed the soon to be released August job numbers. The prevailing opinion was that any report in which the 8.3% unemployment rate inched up or remained the same would be bad news for President Obama coming off the high of the convention. Then the numbers were released – 96,000 new jobs with a lowered unemployment rate of 8.1% - and the immediate reaction was that these were really disappointing numbers for the President.

But wait! Did everyone just completely miss the fact that it was the Republicans who had sat on the President's jobs and infrastructure projects for a year, refused to pass them? Could their memories be that short, or was this just another example of the media arbitrarily picking its winners and losers with no factual basis.

After all, the President and Congress are needed to get the job done in Washington. So why weren't these, also, disappointing numbers for Congress and specifically Republicans who prevented jobs being created by the President?

Poverty, Politics and Race (The View From Down Here)

States under the control of GOP Governors and Legislatures further exacerbated the situation with thousands of public sector layoffs at the state level to drive up unemployment numbers.

Romney even chided Florida's Republican Governor, Rick Scott, for proudly announcing job growth instead of sticking to the party line of a dismal job record due to Obama's policies. These media representatives were also well aware of the Republicans' lies about Obama's record and their hypocrisy in decrying the stimulus for having created no jobs, while being among the first in line with requests for stimulus dollars for projects to create jobs in their own states.

From where I sat, 96,000 new jobs and a lowered unemployment rate from 8.3% to 8.1% was clearly moving in the right direction and good news to me. It's simple arithmetic, as former President Bill Clinton stated so well. Americans understand simple Math.

My Mom used to tell us – "As Black people, we can't just be good at what we do. We must be the best just to be considered worthy." That seems to be the standard to which President Obama is held.

And as often as the media repeated that there was a major enthusiasm gap among Democrats for the President going into the November election, they were wrong. Thousands of Democrats who look like the America I know and love crowded into that arena in Charlotte in September 2012 and proved their satisfaction and

Poverty, Politics and Race (The View From Down Here)

enthusiasm throughout the convention for nominating Barack Obama their standard bearer for a second term as our President. He has proven himself from his first day in office worthy of that support. He had earned it through an unmatched record of hard work on behalf of Americans.

And there were fair-minded Americans of every race, ethnicity, gender and age who left that convention ready to fight for a man who had spent four hard years fighting for them – against the greatest odds imaginable. If any President deserved a second term, it was Barack Obama. The Lord knows he had earned it.

Poverty, Politics and Race (The View From Down Here)

Chapter 15

Politicizing the U.S. Supreme Court

Poverty, Politics and Race (The View From Down Here)

Chief Justice John Roberts' vote in favor of the Obama Administration's Healthcare Reform Act and the announcement of the U.S. Supreme Court's 5 to 4 position on June 28, 2012 sent shock waves through both the GOP and Democrats alike. It was the first time the GOP railed angrily against a decision of the Supreme Court they thought could be counted upon to vote reliably the conservative line. After all, President Reagan's appointees Scalia and Kennedy, and President George W. Bush's appointees Thomas, Alito, and Roberts formed the conservative majority on the 2012 U.S. Supreme Court.

The Democrats were equally in shock, but pleasantly so, because almost no one expected Roberts - generally considered among the most conservative chief justices – to vote with the more liberal minority to uphold one of the key accomplishments of President Obama's first term. The Chief Justice's vote and decision to write the prevailing opinion lent credibility to "Obamacare" in the eyes of the public for a program that had been under attack by the right since introduced by the President 3 year earlier.

It was the common opinion by Democrats that the Court was rigged with the most right wing, conservative majority in the history of the court – with the exception that Justice Kennedy, on rare occasions, voted with the more liberal Justices Ginsberg, Breyer, Sotomayer, and Kagan, appointed by Presidents Clinton and Obama. It was, as a matter of fact, a going wager that if the vote went President Obama's way, Kennedy would be the

Poverty, Politics and Race (The View From Down Here)

deciding vote instead of Chief Justice Roberts. As it turned out, Kennedy wrote a scathing minority opinion. Generally, most Supreme Court watchers and political pundits had predicted that Obama's Affordable Care Act would be struck down in part – the "mandate" – or altogether.

To put everything in proper perspective, it is important to recount the extreme conservatism of the Roberts Court that produced the Citizens United ruling, unleashing unlimited corporate money into the political arena under the guise of free speech.

First, Scalia and Thomas are easily considered among the most extreme right wing partisans on the Supreme Court. They have been so reliably conservative that very few progressives ever expect them to act in any way except in rigid compliance to the Republican Party line. There is justification for this belief from their past behavior.

Scalia showed his true colors in 2001. Scalia was fully aware that a lawsuit by the Sierra Club and Judicial Watch, challenging the Bush administration's Executive Order preventing the release of the membership list for Vice President Cheney's secret energy advisory committee, was scheduled before the Supreme Court. Even with this case pending before the Court, Scalia accepted an invitation from Cheney to join him on a hunting trip, fully funded by Cheney and the U.S. government, including travel on a government plane.

Poverty, Politics and Race (The View From Down Here)

Though this cast doubt on Scalia's judgment and impartiality, it did not impact his decision to take the trip with his good friend, then Vice President Dick Cheney – a party to the Sierra Club case. Further, Associate Justice Scalia refused to recuse himself from participation in the review and vote on the case. The Supreme Court ruled in favor of the Bush administration. This permitted Cheney and the Bush team to continue a pattern that allowed corporate entities regulated by government to write the rules and policies for which they were expected to comply. To the average American following the case, it seemed a lot like the fox guarding the hen house.

And if that was not bad enough, Scalia went on to make speeches declaring that Guantanamo detainees are not entitled to legal protection under the U.S. Constitution's equal protection clause of the 14th Amendment. This was an incredible statement by a sitting Supreme Court Justice, since judges are prohibited from advocacy on issues to protect the impartiality of the judicial system. And second, the Supreme Court had ruled unanimously in 1971 that such rights are protected.

Then, there is Associate Justice Clarence Thomas whose nomination was confirmed by the U.S. Senate in a swirl of scandal that left little doubt in the minds of many American women that we had few rights he felt obligated to protect. Since, he has continued a pattern of scandal and controversy. Thomas' wife was employed by the Heritage Foundation – very vocally opposed to public funding of healthcare, the Dream Act

Poverty, Politics and Race (The View From Down Here)

Immigration Reform, women's reproductive and abortion rights, and any changes to the tax code that would increase taxes for the wealthy. Though Virginia Thomas earned close to $700,000 between 2003 and 2007 in her position with the Heritage Foundation and was a vocal advocate on the group's policy positions before Republican and Tea Party audiences, Justice Thomas failed to disclose her income and the source in repeated filings with the IRS. Thomas, an Associate Justice for the highest court in the land, claimed he "inadvertently omitted" the information due to a misunderstanding of the filing instructions". Yeah.

Likewise, Thomas himself has pulled in speaker fees before exclusively Republican/Conservative groups – clearly sharing his opinion on issues on which the Supreme Court has acted or are scheduled to be before the Court. Salon.com reported that before the high court's controversial decision on the Citizens United case, Thomas took an all expense paid trip in 2008 to Palm Springs for 4 days to attend political strategy and fundraising seminars hosted by Koch Industries.

Thomas's 2008 financial disclosure forms indicated that his transportation, lodging, and meal expenses were paid by the Federalist Society for the 4 days of the conference. The Koch brothers, owners of Koch Industries worth $100 billion, were also sponsors of the Citizens United case before the Supreme Court. Common Cause challenged both Thomas and Scalia's trip, paid for by a party involved in a case before the court. It seemed a clear

Poverty, Politics and Race (The View From Down Here)

conflict of interest and violation of judicial ethics. Both justices were asked to recues themselves. Neither did so.

The vote was 5-4 on this landmark case allowing corporations to spend an unlimited amount of money in political campaigns without disclosing the source. The Koch brothers spent millions of dollars in support of Mitt Romney's campaign to defeat President Obama, as well as other high profile Republican races throughout the country. Had Scalia and Thomas fairly disclosed their conflict and refrained from voting on this issue, the Citizens United case would not have had the votes to proceed.

Thomas's conflict was far worse. His wife had been employed by the Heritage Foundation for four years, earning $700,000, and continued to be affiliated with the organization once her employment ended. The Heritage Foundation is funded by the Koch brothers, parties in the Supreme Court case. At the same time, Thomas was attending and speaking at these Koch brothers sponsored events with all expenses paid by folks who had a direct interest in the outcome of the case on which Thomas would rule.

By contrast, Justice Elena Kagan, the former Solicitor General in President Obama's Justice Department, responsible for supervising and conducting litigation before the U.S. Supreme Court, recused herself when the Obama administration's challenge to the Arizona Immigration Law reached the Supreme Court. She

Poverty, Politics and Race (The View From Down Here)

obviously has a deeper respect for the integrity of the Court and the Code of Ethics for U.S. Judges than at least two of her colleagues. That code states that judges have a responsibility "to act at all times in a manner that promotes public confidence in the integrity and impartiality of the judiciary, and avoid impropriety and the appearance of impropriety in all activities".

Clearly, Scalia and Thomas feel none of these rules apply to them, leaving them free to elevate their personal politics above their duty to dispense justice in an impartial manner, while preserving the integrity of America's third branch of government. Unfortunately, there is no recourse for the American people to require compliance if the Justices' own conscience does not move them to comply.

These two Justices have demonstrated an alarming disrespect for their oath to "administer justice without respect to persons, and do equal right to the poor and to the rich, and ... faithfully and impartially discharge and perform all the duties incumbent upon (them) under the Constitution and laws of the United States". As a result, the court has dramatically changed the face of politics by giving almost total power to the rich, and providing little protection for the free speech rights of all other Americans in the political process.

The conduct of Scalia and Thomas demonstrates alarmingly the importance of who is in the White House when the next appointment is made to the Supreme Court. Existing examples of

Poverty, Politics and Race (The View From Down Here)

extreme partisanship, and allegiance to a Republican agenda that seeks to roll back rights guaranteed to all Americans, make it more critical than ever that new appointees to the court are more similar to Kagan than the ultra political Scalia and Thomas.

Chapter 16

Voter Suppression – An Assault on Democracy

Poverty, Politics and Race (The View From Down Here)

Not since the Jim Crow laws of the 1950's and 60's has there been such an all out war against voter rights as we have seen launched by the Republican Party in 2011-2012. The GOP had obviously decided though they had thrown everything at President Obama except the kitchen sink, it would be difficult to beat the President in a fair fight for the White House in 2012. So every state with a Republican Governor and Republican-controlled Legislature introduced or successfully passed laws between 2011 and 2012 that placed more rigid restrictions on requirements for voter registration and in-person voting. It seemed their plan was to prevent certain voter participation by making it as difficult as possible – particularly for the poor and minorities. If that failed, a law requiring a specific type of voter ID, difficult to obtain before the next election, would frustrate and disenfranchise registered voters who fit the profile of an Obama likely voter.

These laws were designed to prevent the registration of new voters and create a roadblock that would suppress voter turnout in 2012 among minorities, the poor, and urban voters – those who were likely to vote Democratic based on demographics most supportive of Obama in 2008. The GOP claimed the purpose for this sudden spat of new laws so close to the 2012 election was to prevent voter fraud.

There was just one problem – even the sponsors of these suppressive laws could produce no evidence of the voter fraud the laws were created to prevent. On the contrary, the facts revealed no in-

Poverty, Politics and Race (The View From Down Here)

person voter fraud that these laws were created specifically to address. Based on U.S. Justice Department data, there have been 140 people charged with election fraud out of almost 146 million registered voters in 2012. Of the 140 charged, 100 were convicted. There have been only 10 cases of the in-person voter impersonation fraud nationally in the 10 years the data was collected, according to a report from the Carnegie-Knight News 21 Program. That amounted to an occurrence rate of "one out of every 15 million voters" based on an article titled "Cases of Voter ID Election Fraud Virtually Non-Existent" by Natasha Khan and Corbin Carson.

Put bluntly, there was clearly no voter fraud epidemic that required Republicans to rush through these laws to severely restrict the voting rights of minorities, poor, urban, and young voters prior to the 2012 election, except as a strategy to help elect Mitt Romney President and win enough seats to retake the U.S. Senate by Republicans. The only purpose for laws that required legally registered, elderly black Americans to obtain birth certificates, often in another state, in order to obtain the newly mandated photo ID was voter suppression pure and simple.

In many of the states, these laws were designed to prohibit the use of the type of photo identification many citizens already had, but specified exceptions for the type ID Republican voters were more likely to possess. For example, Republicans are strongly supported by the National Rifle Association (NRA) and gun advocates; so the

Poverty, Politics and Race (The View From Down Here)

GOP made sure that gun licenses were accepted as valid ID.

In the 2008 Presidential election, young voters came out in record numbers to support Obama, and were credited in large part with his victory; both as voters and technology savvy, enthusiastic volunteers. It was, therefore, no surprise that many of these voter suppression laws ruled that student photo ID did not qualify as an acceptable voter ID.

The Jim Crow laws of the 19th and 20th century in the American South that used poll taxes, literacy tests, and violence to deny the vote to Black Americans and ensure they would have no say in the government controlling their lives. It was after the reconstruction era that the former confederacy constructed a legal system that institutionalized the separation of the White race from people of color in every area of life – housing, schools, jobs, restaurants, entertainment and recreation, churches, public facilities, hospitals, and even cemeteries.

To maintain White supremacy and exclude Black citizens from access to the governmental process, special laws were passed to ensure Blacks were denied citizenship rights and the vote. The worst examples were the Poll Tax and special Literacy Tests designed to ensure failure for Black residents, while providing exemptions for White residents from these voter restrictions.

Poverty, Politics and Race (The View From Down Here)

The Poll Tax required residents to pay a fee to be allowed to register to vote – and exercise their citizenship rights under the Constitution granted with the passage of the 14th Amendment, passed by Congress in 1866 and ratified in 1868. It was the Thirteenth Amendment passed in 1864 by the Senate and in 1864 by the House, however, that outlawed slavery. Until then, the Dred Scott Decision by the U.S. Supreme Court in 1857 had made it clear that all Blacks_ whether slave or free_ were not covered by the U.S. Constitution.

Dred Scott, a freed slave, had appealed to the Supreme Court, when he moved from a free state to the slave state of Missouri, to grant him freedom. Chief Justice Roger B. Taney issued the majority opinion on behalf of the Court stating that as a Black man, Scott neither had citizenship rights or even the standing to sue. The Justice added that Blacks...

"...had no rights which the White man was bound to respect; and that the negro might justly and lawfully be reduced to slavery for his benefit. He was bought and sold and treated as an ordinary article of merchandise and traffic, whenever profit could be made of it".

Taney further declared that Blacks were excluded from the phrase in the Declaration of Independence that stated, "All men are created equal" in the following quote from his opinion. "It is too clear for dispute that the enslaved African race were not intended to be included, and formed no part of the people who framed and adopted this declaration."

Poverty, Politics and Race (The View From Down Here)

It seems today, a very different Republican Party than President Lincoln's is hell bent on a return to laws of those early days in our history.

The Citizenship Clause of the Fourteenth Amendment went further than the Thirteenth Amendment conferring on Blacks the rights of citizenship, due process, and equal protection for all persons born or naturalized in the United States. Black Americans were finally granted citizenship rights. The Fifteenth Amendment, ratified in 1870, prohibited each government in the United States from denying a citizen the right to vote based on race, color, or previous condition of servitude.

Bitter over the passage of the 13th, 14th, and 15th Amendments to the Constitution, White politicians in southern states passed what became known as "Jim Crow" laws to preserve the separation of the races – "separate but equal" laws. Actually, circumstances were very unequal. That situation was not corrected until after the passage of the Civil Rights and Voting Rights Acts in 1964 and 1965.

Literacy Tests took many forms. Some required impossible requirements of guessing the number of small items in a large glass jar to answering a long list of questions about the U.S. Constitution accurately, for which White citizens were exempted. Those Blacks who passed the test were then faced with threats or actual beatings when they attempted to register to vote. These Jim Crow laws were passed under "State Rights" as a maneuver around strict adherence to the amended

Poverty, Politics and Race (The View From Down Here)

U.S. Constitution, allowing Southern states cover to say they were complying with federal law, when in actuality they continued the same pattern of segregation under their so-called separate but equal laws.

The 13th, 14th, and 15th amendments to the Constitution put into law the abolition of slavery and the guarantee of citizenship and voting rights for Black Americans. Today's calls by Tea Party activists and the Republican Party to get the federal government out of states' business and return most federal decisions and programs to the authority of states is the GOP's veiled campaign to return to the racism of the past under Jim Crow laws and States' Rights. The Republican campaign to declare current registered voters ineligible to vote if they do not possess the newly required state-issued voter ID is a clear example of the Jim Crow tactics employed by Southern states between Reconstruction and the 1960's in the U.S.

For those who pretend not to understand how requiring a specific state –issued voter ID presents any real difficulty for anyone who wants to vote, the following should enlighten them. The Alabama voter ID law requires Alabama residents to produce a birth certificate, passport, driver's license, state issued non-driver ID, naturalization documents, or proof of citizenship from the federal government. This may not seem so onerous to the average upper or middle income American because they likely have easy access to one or more of these documents in their possession. However, for low-income residents of urban inner cities or rural

Poverty, Politics and Race (The View From Down Here)

communities, who have no car and will likely never have a need for a passport, the costs are prohibitive and require an added financial burden when they already have so little for basic family needs. And a passport, naturalization papers, and federal proof of citizenship can take months for issue, making it impossible for a new voter registration applicant to register in time to vote in an approaching election.

Elderly, poor Americans who may have been born outside of a medical facility decades ago would find it almost impossible to obtain an official birth record other than notes in the family Bible, rendering them ineligible to register or unable to vote – if already registered – without a birth certificate to qualify for a government issued photo ID. Further, enacting such laws within months before the 2012 election did not provide adequate time for millions of Americans to complete the processing for a voter ID even if they could afford it by Election Day, with laws taking effect so close to the date of the election. Rural poor face both financial and transportation barriers to obtaining such identification to vote. Requiring poor, elderly, minority, and young Americans to pay sometimes very high fees compared to their limited income, even when they are already legally registered to vote – is just a 21st century version of the Poll Tax.

However, voter suppression tactics were not limited to just voter ID laws. Other strategies included voter purges from eligible voter lists by Republican Secretaries of State and requiring voters to prove their names shouldn't have been removed – a particularly sinister practice since

Poverty, Politics and Race (The View From Down Here)

these chief state elections officers are charged with ensuring fair access to the voting process rather than restricting it. It reminds me of Katherine Harris, the Florida Republican Secretary of State who was also George W. Bush's state campaign advisor in 2000. She seemed to completely forget her statutory obligation to ensure fair, honest elections for the state's citizens; and instead focused on doing whatever necessary to ensure the election of George W. Bush in her campaign role – a good argument for making state election officials non-partisan and prohibiting their involvement in campaigns.

Other tactics included the elimination or shortening of the time frame for in person early voting in some states that favored Democrats. The youth vote went heavily for Obama in 2008 and was likely to do the same in 2012. In 2012, polls showed Obama was more likely to take a majority of the Black, Latino/ Hispanic, and female vote, as well. Pennsylvania restricted perfectly acceptable photo identification used in the past such as U.S. military ID, employee photo ID, university ID, and city or county ID. Absolutely ridiculous and unnecessary. Further, in states with Republican governors, the rules were change and made much more difficult for restoration of rights including voting rights. Stated goals at the time of release of ex-offenders should be to enroll them in re-entry programs for successful re-entry into the community, rather than recidivism.. That's why in some states, those who have paid their dues to society – particularly for non-violent crimes – have their citizenship rights

Poverty, Politics and Race (The View From Down Here)

automatically restored upon release. That is as it should be in every state.

Former Florida Governor Charlie Crist, then a moderate Republican, had reformed the state's program to make it easy for rights restoration for non-violent ex-offenders, and a more lengthy application and review process for more serious offenses. When Rick Scott became the Florida Governor in 2010, the clock was turned back decades by making ex-offender citizenship rights almost impossible to achieve.

A repeatedly used example of how suppressive these laws is 93 year old Pennsylvania resident, Viviette Applewhite, who sued over the law that would have denied her the right to vote. Her first vote was for John F. Kennedy. She had been adopted and was unable to obtain an official birth certificate required for the new Voter ID. Her purse had also been stolen with her social security card and other identification. With the help of the ACLU she fought back. Her case had brought on such a great deal bad publicity to the Pennsylvania law that the state waived the required documentation and issued a Voter ID to Ms. Applewhite.

The Pennsylvania House Majority Leader, Mike Turzai (R. Allegheny), made it clear why the Republican sponsored Voter ID law was so necessary in a speech to the Republican State Committee. He stated, "Pro-Second Amendment? Castle Doctrine, it's done. First pro-life legislation, done... Voter ID, which is going to allow Governor

Poverty, Politics and Race (The View From Down Here)

Romney to win the state of Pennsylvania, done". Finally the truth! The utter disruption of millions of Americans' right to vote came down to a Republican Party so intent on paving the way for Mitt Romney to win Pennsylvania's electoral votes, even if dishonestly, that the harm they did to innocent Americans, our Constitution, and the state's citizens meant nothing to them.

Mary Sanchez, with the Kansas City Star, wrote in her article titled "Will Republicans succeed with Jim Crow lite laws" stated the following in reference to the rash of Voter ID Laws.

"Old Southern political bosses of the Jim Crow era would have winked in delight at the ingenious ploys of their latter day successors in the art of voter suppression".

Unless they were Americans living in caves in some remote part of the country, there was little doubt that the purpose of these racist laws was for voter suppression among democratic leaning voters – motivated by partisan Republican politics. The Brennan Center for Justice reported:

"State governments across the country enacted an array of new laws making it harder to register or to vote. Some states require voters to show government issued photo identification, often of a type that as many as one in ten voters do not have. Other states have cut back on early voting...Two states reversed earlier reforms and once again disenfranchised millions who have past criminal convictions but who are now taxpaying members of

Poverty, Politics and Race (The View From Down Here)

the community. Still others made it much more difficult for citizens to register to vote."

The report noted that the cumulative impact of these laws (1.) made it significantly harder for over 5 million Americans to vote in the crucial 2012 election; (2.) eliminated early voting the weekend before the election very important to poor and minority voters; (3.) created unnecessary requirements to qualify for the government-issued photo ID that specifically targeted college-aged students, poor, and minority citizens; (4.) purged legal voters from the voter rolls at the eleventh hour; and (5.) added a financial burden to obtaining the new voter ID similar to the poll tax of the past.

Poor people should never be forced to use their limited income to pay for the right to vote – that should be already guaranteed under the Constitution at no cost except their citizenship as an American.

It would be hilarious if it was not so serious and dangerous to our democracy that the very same Republican Party that set off this Voter ID bomb to prevent voter fraud turns out to be the source of the only voter fraud discovered leading into the 2012 election. As it turns out, the Republican National Committee paid Strategic Allied Consulting owned by Nathan Sproul over $3 million for get-out-the vote efforts in 7 swing states. The voter registration effort in Palm Beach Florida revealed addresses on many of the voter registration forms were for gas stations and other business or non-residential locations. Sproul's registration campaign in Nevada

Poverty, Politics and Race (The View From Down Here)

resulted in more scandal. Reports were ripped up and thrown away. One must wonder if the GOP worker was instructed to fill in the party affiliations requested to be left blank with the Republican Party. Further, in Palm Beach, Florida the Supervisor of Elections found that the same handwriting was evident in the signatures on many of the voter registration forms – with strong implications that the names on the forms were fraudulently signed by the campaign/get-out-the-vote worker. A Florida Department of Law Enforcement (FDLE) investigation was launched based on allegations of this voter registration scam in up to ten counties in Florida. With allegations emerging in Nevada with the same Sproul Company, criminal charges should have followed.

Sean Spicer, spokesman for the RNC, said the Party had "zero tolerance" for voter fraud, as he announced the Republican National Committee had fired Sproul and his company. However, when the GOP hired him they already were well aware of his checkered past. Sproul was a known, longtime Republican operative who got himself in the same kind of trouble during the 2004 election. Though Spicer tried to paint this as just the work of one paid field worker, that story obviously was not true since the same problems occurred in 10 Florida counties and was documented in Nevada. Some of those who were registering voters required people to answer the question – "Who are you voting for in the Presidential election?" – a violation of non-partisan, non-political rules of voter registration efforts.

Poverty, Politics and Race (The View From Down Here)

This is a company famous for shredding Democratic voter registrations and only turning in those registered as Republicans. Proof that the RNC were aware of Sproul's shady past practices was the fact that RNC officials required him to change the name of his company to Strategic Allied Consulting to hide his association with his other companies swamped in this same kind of scandal in 2004. The RNC did not fire him because of zero tolerance for voter fraud. They fired him because he got caught. Further, it was likely unless these most recent schemes landed him in jail, Sproul would continue to be a player in the Republican Party – and not as a minor player. He, after all, was listed among Mitt Romney's campaign consultants in 2012, according to a report by David Babash.

The current Republican Party is devoid of the morals on which they judge all other Americans. The Republican Party of Mitt Romney and Ryan have lied so much and played so fast and loose with facts and the truth during the 2012 campaign that they would not recognize the truth if they had a head-on collision with it. It, therefore, is no surprise that they would preside over a party as dishonest and disrespectful toward the American people and the U.S. Constitution as these frauds clearly demonstrated.

America deserves much better than they offer. Further, Americans deserve better than the Jim Crow laws of another time – a time that America was lifting itself out of one of the most shameful periods in our history, slavery.

Poverty, Politics and Race (The View From Down Here)

The long lines during the 2012 election caused by the law that cut the amount of days allowed for early voting.

Chapter 17

The Death of News

Poverty, Politics and Race (The View From Down Here)

In 2012 I finally gave up and swore off so-called "news" shows, and just accepted that real investigative news reporting had become as extinct as the dinosaur. After repeated calls to the CNN comment line with warnings that they were at great risk of losing the title as "the place for news", I simply stopped watching for a long period. It had become just another click on my TV remote for talking heads, spouting political spin and mostly unsubstantiated opinion. I wanted old fashioned, unadulterated, objective reporting of the facts on current events that allowed me to form my own opinions.

However, it seemed CNN the cable station that built its reputation on 24 hour news coverage, had given up on its primary mission. Though I enjoyed the steady diet of political talkers on television and radio, I had come to depend on CNN as my main source for news - factual, objective reporting on important events of the day. Unfortunately, in recent years, CNN has made the choice to give up hard hitting, investigative news reporting to concentrate almost completely on current event and political commentary. Their former award winning, in depth news coverage had been co-opted by repetitious interruptions of canned announcement masquerading as news.

It is not the standard of excellence to which we had become accustomed. Likewise, it dishonored the reputations of past, veteran journalists whose commitment to their professions made CNN such a credible source of news.

Poverty, Politics and Race (The View From Down Here)

Of course, the half hour dose of national news on the major TV networks ABC, CBS, and NBC provide good "hit and run" coverage. However, 30 to 60 seconds hardly counts as substantive, in depth coverage on complex issues that impact our daily lives. And national news coverage in daily or weekly newspapers – for those that have not already gone under – is so thin that only two pages would be needed if not for sports, entertainment, style and arts sections, ads and coupons. Further, with the dominance of the internet and the availability of round the clock updates on national and international issues, the daily newspaper has little value except as a local news source. And for rural communities with newspapers published weekly, the news is actually history by the time the newspaper reaches the reader. However, as a source of information on local issues, activities, services, and events, it still serves a valuable purpose.

Without a vigilant and independent news media _committed to high standards of journalistic ethics to inform, educate and serve as the public's major protection against corruption, there is no objective filter to distinguish fact from fiction in the massive amounts of garbage we are exposed to every day. Such a situation provides an opening for the likes of the FOX News Network to take itself serious as a legitimate news source.

With no fact checking, the GOP has been free to run rough shod over the rights of most Americans while using the public's lack of facts about the issues to convince them to vote against their own interests. Lies, misrepresentations of the

Poverty, Politics and Race (The View From Down Here)

facts, and half truths, unchallenged by good news reporting to unveil the imposters, has led to the takeover of Congress by some of the most extreme factions in our country.

They have brought great harm to our country by putting their political agendas ahead of healing gaping wounds to America's economy, and destroyed even the semblance of civility in Washington and the country toward solving our most pressing problems. With impunity, these Republican Party extremists have interfered with or blocked efforts to pass infrastructure, jobs, education, consumer protection, needed regulatory and tax reform legislation; and even prevented the approval of cabinet positions, federal judges, and the budget to allow the federal government to carry out the important day to day business of this country. In 2011, they almost did irreparable damage to the economy and our financial standing in the world when they refused to approve an increase in the debt ceiling within a breath of financial default. Worse, this abuse of power continued, without fear of exposure, because the news media had become such a "paper tiger" either out of fear of being labeled the liberal media, laziness, or fear of litigation. However, truth is the best defense against a successful lawsuit, and the best way to ensure a credible media.

It is not hard to find examples of this abuse and hypocrisy. The Republican led House of Representatives blocked every attempt by the President and Democrats to create more jobs by voting overwhelmingly against President Obama's

Poverty, Politics and Race (The View From Down Here)

American Jobs Act, and Infrastructure Bill to put Americans to work rebuilding crumbling, unsafe roads and bridges throughout the country, while railing against Obama for failing in his promise to create jobs. Republican House leaders like Ryan, Canter, and Boehner brazenly appeared on national news shows decrying Democrats for doing nothing to correct high unemployment rates, after killing the very programs that would have created the jobs to reduce unemployment in America. This was key to the GOP's stated plan to deny America's first Black President any successes in his first term in order to deny him a second term; regardless of the harm it caused the country.

With full knowledge of the GOP's sabotage of the President's efforts to rebuild the nation's economy, "news" organizations never confronted this fraud with timely reporting to expose the damage they were doing to our country to exact political retribution against President Obama. Instead, CNN handled the situation as though it was a political debate, giving each side the opportunity to comment and respond; treating lies, and almost criminal negligence, like casual differences of opinion. Even experienced, smart journalists like MSNBC's Chuck Todd continued to confront only the President and Democrats with the question, "Why is it taking so long for the economy to recovery?" as if only Democrats have responsibility for our country's economic condition.

Most inside the Beltway journalist understand very well how we got into this recession and which Party took us there. The President

Poverty, Politics and Race (The View From Down Here)

accountable for this mess was George W. Bush, with a Republican Party in control of the Congress. And the media's willingness to ignore the Republican controlled House's responsibility for blocking every attempt by President Obama and the Democratic Senate to heal the economy removes any claim of impartiality by the media.

Further, there did not seem a realistic understanding that no one could immediately correct an economy in free fall and in the worse condition since the Great Depression; even if both parties had been working in concert. The Great Depression began with the stock market crash in 1929 and most economists and historians agree that our country did not recover until 1941, 12 years later. Therefore it is ridiculous that the media bought into this GOP premise that President Obama alone was responsible for correcting the huge mess, in less than 4 years, which George Bush handed off to him in January 2009. Why weren't Ryan, Boehner, Canter, and McConnell confronted regularly about their obstructionist behavior that blocked the infrastructure Bill, the American Jobs Act, voted against the American Recovery and Reinvestment Act and limited the size of the stimulus, all of which would have added millions more jobs and put recovery on a faster track? The right question was not whether Americans were better off than 4 years ago, but rather who prevented a faster recovery for America. The resounding answer would have been the Republican Party.

Poverty, Politics and Race (The View From Down Here)

This kind of fact free reporting was to be expected of the Fox News Network, which openly acted as though they were the communications arm of the Republican Party. However, we had come to expect more from those who took pride in the journalistic profession. When elected leaders, charged with upholding the highest ethical standards in carrying out the business of the country, lie and betray the public's trust, we expect a fair and objective media to keep them honest by exposing such behavior in fair news coverage.

Those of us who expected that kind of vigilance from the news media were disappointed. And instead, Republicans were allowed to do their dirt unimpeded, while presenting a false face to the public of their concern for the millions of unemployed Americans, families left homeless due to mortgage foreclosures, businesses on the brink of closure, and local and state governments operating in deficit due to the state of the economy.

The Republican refrain during the 2012 presidential election was the admission that the President inherited a bad economy; but, with the lie that "he made it worse". They were fully aware that it was the Republican Congress that deliberately made the economy worse by refusing to allow a vote on many of President Obama's stimulus programs by abusing the filibuster. If not for the smart talkers on shows like MSNBC's **Rachel Maddow, The Last Word with Lawrence O'Donnell**, and internet reports like the Huffington Post, we would likely still be in the dark on the breadth and depth of these offenses against the American public by

Poverty, Politics and Race (The View From Down Here)

Republicans. The obligation of a journalist is to provide the facts that allow a discerning public to separate truth from fiction, instead of just accepting the lie. By not challenging even the most blatant lies, the media gave tacit approval and allowed them to be repeated over and over until they took on the appearance of truth; a major disservice to both the media's mission and the public.

That is how the "Death Panel" myth about President Obama's Healthcare Reform Act, widely repeated by GOP leaders and Tea Party activist, took on a life of its own. Supporters of Healthcare Reform were caught totally off guard by this line of attack because it just did not seem plausible that anyone, no matter how uninformed, would actually believe their government would conspire to kill off older Americans. However, as incredible as it was, with no push back on this ridiculous lie from the news media, that became the most memorable argument against healthcare reform for those opposed to extending healthcare to the over 45 million Americans without affordable access.

The "birther theory", an absolutely insane rumor that Obama's parents somehow conspired to manipulate newborn Barack Obama's birth certificate to hide a Kenyan, instead of his actual Hawaiian birth, so that four decades later he could run for President is another lie that got completely out of hand before pressure was put on the media to debunk this lie. Unfortunately, by then the myth had already become legend in the minds of so many Americans that more than half of Republicans polled claimed they believed or were unsure

Poverty, Politics and Race (The View From Down Here)

whether Obama was born in Kenya; and therefore an illegitimate occupant of the White House. It was only under pressure from challenges to this foolish theory by MSNBC hosts like Chris Matthews that news organizations finally tried to knock down this false public perception. For months they had, instead, treated this craziness as though it had the right to be taken seriously, even after they had undeniable evidence of the President's birth place through his official Hawaiian birth certificate and newspaper birth announcement.

Even three years later, with almost universal acceptance by fair-minded Americans that the "Birther Theory" was a ridiculous fraud, most in the media were unwilling to admit that the refusal of these extremists to accept the legitimacy of Obama's election was race-based, not issues oriented. The attacks were not on any specific issue, but rather sought to have the President disqualified on the basis of his birth due to the U.S. citizenship requirement. Claiming Obama was born in Kenya, if they succeeded, would not only have made him ineligible to be President, but the scandal would have completely erased this history making election of the first African-American President altogether.

It was as though the perpetrators of this fraud had no idea that no one is confirmed in the most important job in the nation without the full background check required for almost any new employee anywhere. That's why it was surprising that a claim this absurd was not immediately fact checked and stopped in its tracks by news organizations that could have quickly made simple

Poverty, Politics and Race (The View From Down Here)

inquiries of federal agencies. Did these Tea Party activists think the Chief Justice of the U.S. Supreme Court would join in such a conspiracy by knowingly swearing in a person disqualified to hold the office of President?

MSNBC, with its team of political experts and nationally known journalists, has become my most trustworthy source of information on politics and current events. The network's hosts look more like America, representing a diversity of ethnicities, ages, and political perspectives. Though Joe Scarborough of **Morning Joe** is a bit overbearing, often bullying and disrespectful toward Mika and guests with whom he disagrees, his show includes commentary that exposes the viewer to varied perspective on issues and the facts behind them.

The daily line up of show hosts includes Joe and Mika in the morning, followed by recognized journalists Chuck Todd and Andrea Mitchell. Then the afternoon starts with Alex Wagner and Tamron Hall, rising stars who objectively report the news and provide a more complete, factual context in which to view the new information; followed by the young gun team on the Cycle, and the smart, witty, and thought provoking Martin Bashir. Now that I'm retired, I finally get the chance to check in on the daytime talkers and follow their perspectives on political decisions affecting my life.

However, no cable network can match the MSNBC evening schedule starting with Chris Matthews who really understands the political landscape. Reverend Al Sharpton brings a fresh

Poverty, Politics and Race (The View From Down Here)

perspective from his many years of civil and human rights activism, followed by the passionate Ed Shultz, and the very smart Rachel Maddow who takes pride in meticulously examining the factual basis for her conclusions; a very scholarly approach. The schedule ends with the consummate political analyst, Lawrence O'Donnell, who seems completely in his element comparing notes on the day's events with guests or debating opposing views with others. The excellent weekend shows, Up with Chris Hayes and Melissa Harris-Perry, keep me intellectually alert and up to date on Saturday and Sunday mornings.

It was through these shows that the public gained access to most of the important political news and had it analyzed from every angle before forming an opinion. I usually tried to check in on CNN; and when I could tolerate it, I would take a short peek at the "fair and balanced" FOX News for a complete context.

Soledad O'Brien is the saving grace for CNN when given the opportunity and flexibility to do investigative reporting. CNN should do more of it. However, during the 2012 election, I did not see much of journalistic excellence in Soledad's "Turning Point" show.

And just when I was becoming very impressed with T.J. Holmes and his willingness to challenge the spin and obvious misrepresentations of the truth by some guests, suddenly he was no longer an on-air host. CNN, with the technological bells and whistles and expert political panels

Poverty, Politics and Race (The View From Down Here)

covering the spectrum of ideologies, gives entertaining election night coverage. Wolf does a good job of facilitating the panel, while John King works his magic with the election maps, projections, results, and the polling behind the results. I only wish CNN would invest as much in high caliber news reporting.

When Republicans in Congress blocked action on President Obama's American Jobs Act which would have pumped $55 billion into communities throughout the U.S. to create jobs and stabilize each state's economy, CNN should have reported that the much needed jobs bill was killed by a Republican filibuster. It would have made it harder for the GOP to then pretend they were the job creators instead of the obstructers.

Likewise, when Republicans railed and voted against Obama's stimulus package as socialist spending, though they understood perfectly that in a recession stimulus is the quickest way to jump start the economy, even voting repeatedly for stimulus spending during Republican administrations, CNN and other real news organizations should have confronted them with their past votes and the hypocrisy. Further, these same Republican leaders should have been blasted publicly by every news organization for voting unanimously against Obama's American Recovery and Reinvestment Act (ARRA) stimulus program while jumping to the front of the line with stimulus requests to spur jobs in their home states. They happily posed for pictures handing over the symbolic cardboard stimulus checks to state

Poverty, Politics and Race (The View From Down Here)

leaders, took credit for the jobs created, and then returned to Washington and joined in the chorus of lies that no jobs were created. At no time did the news media accurately push back against these lies with the truth that Obama's stimulus created millions of jobs.

Even today they have been able to get away with that lie throughout the Republican convention and into the 2012 presidential election because the news media did not step in and confront them with the facts immediately.

It was not the 24-hour coverage on CNN that broke the news that on January 20, 2009, during President Obama's inauguration celebration, the GOP leadership met and pledged to deny the new President any success on his proposed programs, cabinet appointments, and federal judicial appointments in order to deny him a second term. It took internet blogs and MSNBC to break the news. Likewise, when Senate Republicans abused the filibuster rule that requires a 60 vote majority for an override to allow issues to come to the Senate floor for an up or down majority vote a record number of times, they should have been exposed by America's free press.

It is imperative that these Republican obstructionists not be allowed to throw rocks and hide their hands by denying votes on programs of great importance to the American people like the Dream Act for a pathway to citizenship for children of immigrants, the Lilly Ledbetter Act for equal pay for women, the new Consumer Protection Agency

Poverty, Politics and Race (The View From Down Here)

and its director, and regulations to prevent another economic doomsday scenario like the one President Obama inherited from George Bush upon being sworn in as the 44 U.S. President in January 2009.

It is as important to call public attention to actions by either party that threaten the rights of Americans already confirmed in the Constitution. It was hard to believe that the Michigan Emergency Manager Law and voter suppression laws passed in at least 21 states did not deserve "Breaking News" status on every news show, considering the wide implications for the erosion of civil and voting rights laws, as well as the democratic foundations on which our country was built. But it was not the traditional news organizations that broke the story on these major encroachments on our freedoms, but internet news venues. And, again, it was left to MSNBC to call broad public attention to these unprecedented invasions on our Constitutional rights. Both issues deserved in depth reporting and analysis to put the public on notice of the dangers of this kind of extremism being allowed to spread unchecked.

The Michigan Emergency Manager Law had the effect of creating a dictatorship in certain cities with similar characteristics. The Republican Governor and Legislature created the law and targeted Benton Harbor, Detroit, Pontiac, and Ecorse for takeovers by Emergency Managers appointed by Governor Rick Snyder. The stated purpose for the Emergency Manager Law was to allow the authority for the Governor to dissolve the locally elected government, and appoint an

Poverty, Politics and Race (The View From Down Here)

Emergency Manager for cities in financial crisis, with unprecedented authority to fire elected officials, reject, modify, or even terminate existing contracts, including collective bargaining and existing employment agreements. The Emergency Manager appointed to take over the Detroit Public School District immediately issued layoff notices to all 5,466 public school teachers. In the city governments targeted, the Managers have acted quickly to fire the members of the city government legally elected by the citizens of the municipality.

Among the facts that are not widely reported are that the governor and legislature created the financial crisis in these communities by drastically cutting state aid and taxing authority for these cities that have very high African-American populations and high poverty rates. Benton Harbor, the first city targeted, has an 89.2% African American population, and a poverty rate of 48.7%. Detroit's African-American population is 82.2% and has a 34.5% poverty rate. Ecorse's population is 87.7% African-Americans with a 32.7% poverty rate; and Pontiac, with a 52.1% African-American population, has a 22.1% poverty rate. Flint Michigan was a later addition to the cities with a Governor appointed Emergency Manager. It has an African-American population of 56.6%, and a poverty rate of 36.6%.

Such a pattern cannot be accidental. With the clearly racist elements obvious in the way this law was structured and being implemented, it was incredulous to me that the residents of these cities were not fighting back in the courts. It, therefore,

Poverty, Politics and Race (The View From Down Here)

renewed my faith in our democratic system of government when a lawsuit was filed by citizens from throughout the state asking that Michigan's Emergency Manager Law be declared unconstitutional. The lawsuit stated that the law "establishes a new form of local government, previously unknown within the United States or the State of Michigan, where the people within local municipalities may be governed by an unelected official who establishes local law by decree".

This unbelievably brazen assault on the principle of representative government by the people and for the people has barely been mentioned in news coverage by the major news organizations. If not for the internet and MSNBC, and in particular Rachel Maddow, the American public would have little knowledge of the power grab and extreme abuse of power by Michigan's Republican state leaders. If the Michigan law is allowed to stand, I fear we will see it replicated in many more Republican controlled states; just as voter suppression laws have been approved in almost half of the 50 states, for no purpose except to intimidate voters and suppress voter turnout among demographics that traditionally vote democratic. Just as with the Emergency Manager Law, minorities, and the poor are harmed most by these laws.

Though the sponsors of voter suppression legislation hid behind the excuses that they were rooting out voter fraud, they failed to produce evidence documenting voter fraud to justify such drastic measures. In the mid eighties when local

Poverty, Politics and Race (The View From Down Here)

governments and universities were creating affirmative action goals for minority participation and enrollment, challenges were brought in court to require disparity studies to prove a history of past discrimination and show there were no other options to achieve the goal before these programs could go into effect. The Emergency Manager and Voter Suppression laws should have been required to meet similar standards before they were allowed to continue. In America, the impetus should be to create laws that provide all citizens easy access to participate in the governmental process, regardless of race, geography, income, or ideological differences.

When there is no credible news media to hold them accountable to the public, they are given deniability for their bad acts that they do not deserve. When more real news is filtered to the public through the comedy and satirical sketches of late night comedians like Jon Stewart, Stephen Colbert, David Letterman, Jimmy Fallon, and Jay Leno, that is a very good sign that traditional news organizations have failed miserably. The comedians also make us laugh and sometimes forget how horribly wrong politics in this country have become.

Unlike Jon Stewart and Stephen Colbert, however, there is nothing entertaining about the way the GOP has been allowed free reign to destroy the lives of middle and low income Americans, while pretending to work in their behalf. In order to get the foot of Republicans, more interested in preserving their power than making our nation strong, off the necks of the American people, news

Poverty, Politics and Race (The View From Down Here)

organizations must become more accountable and show greater integrity in reporting the news accurately, thoroughly, and objectively.

So, as GOP leaders continue to claim voter suppression laws and purges are requirements to prevent voter fraud where no fraud exists, the news media has an obligation to report the real fraud being committed against the public. When a Republican Secretary of State, charged with ensuring fair and impartial elections, instead imposes rules that are more favorable only in Republican districts or precincts, and less favorable for Democratic voting districts as in Ohio, the news media has an obligation to expose these violations of voter rights.

When Republicans pull out all the stops to ensure the economy and job prospects do not improve for their own political advantage, with little concern for the devastation to unemployed and impoverished Americans, it is the news media's job to expose this callous disregard. And every time the Congressional Republicans vote in lock step to maintain or increase tax breaks for millionaires and billionaires – or to extend subsidies to wealthy oil companies_ while recommending cuts in funding to feed hungry children, poor families, and the elderly, the media does a disservice to the public if it spends its energy handicapping the political race instead of reporting these facts.

It is an important news story that the rich "job creators", who have benefited from two decades of favorable tax laws, deregulation, and high paid

Poverty, Politics and Race (The View From Down Here)

lobbyists to buy as much influence as they could want, have become filthy rich, sat on their wealth, and refused to create jobs. This served to widen the income gap between the wealthy few and the other 99% of Americans who languish near the bottom of the income ladder. If not for the Occupy Wall Street movement, that dramatically shined a light on the growing disparity between the haves and have nots in America, it is doubtful that the plight of poor and middle-income Americans would have received meaningful coverage. And the media would have continued to go along with GOP talking points that the rich had to be made super rich before any jobs could trickle down to the little people.

The Republican Party has been very skillful over recent years in tricking many Americans into believing the interests of the wealthy are also in their best interest. That may have been true in a long gone era before greed became the most prominent value of those who control the country's wealth. And it is the job of the serious journalist, with pride in this honored profession, to tell the truth and stop enabling these bad actors to continue to do harm to our country.

There is no such thing as political correctness with objective reporting of the news. There are no sides. There is just honest reporting of the facts to separate truth from lies. And it is imperative that honest and vigilant news organizations confront lies immediately; not after they have been repeated unchecked so often that they become part of the public's consciousness, and can be mistaken for the truth.

Poverty, Politics and Race (The View From Down Here)

I have a granddaughter who will soon graduate from Florida A&M University with a degree in journalism. It would be a great source of pride to know she is joining a profession that has worked to regain the credibility of its past.

Poverty, Politics and Race (The View From Down Here)

Final Thoughts

The 2012 Election

Poverty, Politics and Race (The View From Down Here)

On election night, I created a no-election news zone around me until the final results were in. I had warned my husband not to share any of the state by state results with me, and set my television on HGTV, Bravo, Everybody Loves Raymond and King of Queens reruns, BET, HBO, or anything that I was sure not to see breaking election news until final results were in. I had taken my blood pressure medication and settled in for a nerve wracking few hours. I even turned off my phone so there would be no calls from family or friends that violated my no play-by-play rule on election night news.

So when my husband called out that I needed to join him quickly – I knew the results were about to be announced. I walked into the room just as all the major TV stations were projecting Obama as the winner in Ohio – taking his electoral vote total over the 270 needed to win the election. All I could do was fall to my knees and say "Thank God!!" It was as though a heavy load had been lifted and I could breathe freely again! I could not even imagine waking up on November 7th to a President Mitt Romney.

Then it was announced that Romney was not going to concede that Obama was the winner in Ohio. My first thought was – God, no. Please not another Florida 2000. Within an hour, however, the Romney team dragged themselves back into reality and Romney made a very gracious, short concession speech soon after. Unbelievably, just one week after the election and his widely praised concession speech, Romney showed his true colors. Reporters, who joined a donor call between Romney and his

Poverty, Politics and Race (The View From Down Here)

national finance committee to explain his loss, released the following Romney comments to the national media.

"The President's campaign focused on giving targeted groups a big gift, especially African-Americans, Hispanics, and young people. In every case they were very generous in what they gave to those groups...you can imagine for somebody making $25,000 or $30,000 or $35,000 a year, being told you're now going to get free health care, particularly if you don't have it, getting free health care worth...what...$10,000 per family in perpetuity, I mean this is huge. Likewise with Hispanic voters, free health care was a big plus. But in addition with regards to Hispanic voters, the amnesty for children of illegals, the so-called Dream Act kids, was a huge plus for that voting group. With regards to young people, for instance, a forgiveness of college loan interest was a big gift. Free contraceptives were very big with young, college-aged women."

He further stated that young people under 26 years old were provided the gift of coverage on their parents' health care plan through Obama care. In other words, his 47% comment during the campaign was no misstatement, though he tried to mislead voters that they were in debates and pre-election speeches. His donor call comments that Obama won because he targeted groups in his base with extraordinary financial gifts from the government and worked aggressively to get them out to vote, sounded a lot like his comments about the 47% of Americans he did not care about who

Poverty, Politics and Race (The View From Down Here)

just wanted others to give them things. And it is proof positive, in case anyone was wondering, that America made the right choice in re-electing President Obama, and soundly rejected Romney. And though my sister-in-law reported two days later that a White woman in the dentist office on November 7 said to the Black woman seated next to her, "I see y'all got your President back in," I was happy to celebrate America for re-electing a President who represents all of America. The President of the United States is just that – the American leader and Commander-in-Chief for this country and every citizen in it. I never understood the GOP rallying cry that they were taking their country back. From whom were they taking it?

Just a week after the President was re-elected, the heads of all of the hate filled right wingers seemed to explode, as they circulated petitions to secede from the United States in protest. Texas, with a population of 25.7 million based on 2011 census data, collected over 100,000 signatures making it doubtful that such a small percentage of the state's population could make that decision on behalf of the other 25.6 million residents of Texas. The chances of the 30,000 petitioners in Florida are just as doubtful; considering Florida's population of 19.1 million and the fact that Obama won both the popular and electoral votes in Florida just a week earlier.

Maybe that's why many of these same Obama haters are starting a campaign to impeach the President that the country had just elected, with no grounds except they hate him so much. If

Poverty, Politics and Race (The View From Down Here)

the Republican Party does not do a better job than Romney of separating themselves from this racist, sexist, homophobic element of their party, they will find themselves moved farther and farther to the political fringe.

President Obama was among only four Presidents in history to win election to both terms by over 50% of the popular vote and an electoral vote landslide – proving all the pundits wrong. Almost to the person, they had declared it would be nearly impossible for Obama to win re-election with an unemployment rate at 7% or above. They were quick to accept GOP spin that the President, alone, was responsible for the state of the economy; as if they forgot the financial disaster George W. Bush handed him and the total obstruction by Republicans in both houses of Congress. It is after all Congress that must approve bills before they can become effective with the President's signature. These supposed smart people acted as if they missed out on basic high school civics.

From the beginning of President Obama's term, the Republicans_ who did not have the votes in Congress to defeat Democratic recommendations for jobs (the American Jobs Act), Healthcare Reform, or the Banking and Wall Street Reform packet_ decided to just obstruct anything the President tried to do to help the country. Fortunately, the House did not have the same rule as the Senate that allows the minority party to filibuster any action by the majority party unless there are 60 out of 100 votes to stop it. Based on that rule, Senate Republicans logged an

Poverty, Politics and Race (The View From Down Here)

unprecedented number of filibusters during the first 3 years of Obama's first term, led by Republican Senate Minority Leader Mitch McConnell.

When Democrats were in the minority, filibusters and cloture votes peaked at 68. Since 2006 when Republicans became the Senate minority party, the filibusters have doubled; peaking at 139 in the two year 2007 and 2008 session of Congress. In many cases they even blocked Democrats being able to bring bills to the floor for debate. Most Americans agree this is a ridiculous rule that allows the minority to prevent the majority from doing the public's business to score political points with their base. It is hoped that when the new session of Congress starts, this will be the first problem to be corrected in order to end this craziness and get on with the real business they were sent to Washington to do.

It was uplifting that most Americans did not buy the Republican or media spin on Obama, as clearly shown by the 2012 election outcome. It was also clear that Obama supporters were not suffering from an enthusiasm gap as polls and media pundits kept saying. The proof is in the fact that voters were so determined to cast their vote for the President they were willing to wait in lines for up to 8 hours in Florida and Ohio – states crucial to victory for both Obama and Romney. That determination was partly due to their anger over GOP voter suppression tactics designed to frustrate and disenfranchise mostly democratic voters.

Poverty, Politics and Race (The View From Down Here)

The other factor was the absolute insistence by Obama supporters that they were not going to allow a President, who had worked so hard to earn re-election under more difficult circumstances than almost any other President, to be defeated. Further, the genius of the Obama campaign, considered one of the best, most strategically effective, political campaigns in history, is that it was constantly identifying new voters through targeted voter registration among new college-aged Americans, Hispanics, Blacks, women, and others who traditionally voted more progressively. At the same time, they cultivated the base by making it a choice election between the President's vision for America rather than an election on the economy alone favoring the wealthy, as Romney hoped and the media predicted.

The media even started singing the refrain from the Romney campaign that Romney would be better able to work across the aisle in actually getting something done in Washington – while there would be the continued stalemate if Obama was re-elected. They were basically saying because recalcitrant Republicans refused to do the people's business in order to prevent Obama getting credit for improving the economy – the public should punish the guy who was in there working hard for us and reward the obstructionists. What a completely ridiculous premise?! The public, however, was smart enough to see through their flimsy arguments.

The Republican Party and their Super PACs tried every under-handed scheme possible to block

Poverty, Politics and Race (The View From Down Here)

President Obama's re-election. The tactics included voter suppression laws, robo-calls to voters with misleading instructions to vote one or two days after the actual election date, to drastically cutting the number of election day polling locations and resources that created long lines to discourage working poor, minority, and young voters who could not afford to wait 3 to 8 hours to vote. The long lines forced students to miss a day of classes, workers to choose between voting or missing several hours of pay that amounted to imposing poll taxes, as during the Jim Crow era. Florida Governor Rick Scott, Ohio Governor John Kasich and Secretary of State Jon Husted, and Colorado's Secretary of State and Chief elections official Scott Gessler were among the worst offenders. And despite all the road blocks they created to deter voters, President Obama won Florida, Ohio, and Colorado – three important "swing states" in his successful re-election.

There were so many questionable tactics by state leaders in Republican controlled Arizona that even a week after the election, provisional ballots were still being counted in order to declare winners in state and Congressional races.

It was, therefore, ironic and highly suspect in this environment that the U.S. Supreme Court chose to take up a challenge from Shelby County Alabama on a key enforcement provision of the 1965 Voting Rights Act. It will be left to history whether a state defined by discrimination, violence, and racism so prominent that it gave birth to the 1964 Civil Rights and 1965 Voting Rights federal laws,

Poverty, Politics and Race (The View From Down Here)

will succeed in eliminating the oversight and enforcement clause that protects the voting rights of millions of Americans.

And while we must be vigilant and cannot afford to take our eyes off the ball, for now I celebrate. I celebrate the fact that President Obama won re-election with one of the broadest coalitions in recent history. According to all post election night analyses, Obama won with a coalition made up of liberal white voters and moderate white women, and record numbers of Black, Latino, Asian, and young voters. The President's winning coalition looked like the melting pot of America and not a replay of the Jim Crow South, where Romney found most of his support.

By soundly defeating the Republican vision that our country is only for and ruled by rich white men, the 2012 election reaffirmed an America that makes my heart swell with pride.

Poverty, Politics and Race (The View From Down Here)